BECOME AN EFFECTIVE TEACHER IN MINUTES:

BEST TEACHING PRACTICES YOU CAN USE NOW

ADAM WAXLER
and
MARJAN GLAVAC

Previously published as an eBook:
eTeach: A Teacher Resource for Learning the Strategies of Master Teachers

© 2019 Marjan Glavac

Title: Become an Effective Teacher in Minutes: Best Teaching Practices You Can Use Now
Format: Paperback
This publication has been assigned: 978-0-9683310-7-1

Title: Become an Effective Teacher in Minutes: Best Teaching Practices You Can Use Now
Format: Electronic book
This publication has been assigned: 978-0-9683310-8-8

Interior Design and Formatting: Ruslan Nabiev

For free resources for getting a teaching job, becoming an effective teacher and making teaching fun, visit:

www.TheBusyEducator.com

Table of Contents

About the Author

Adam landed his first teaching job at Springs Middle School in East Hampton, New York. At Springs, Adam was given free reign to run the middle school social studies department as he wished. He worked quickly to revamp their outdated program, moving away from the textbook-based, teacher-driven social studies curriculum to a more student-centered, constructivist curriculum.

Adam's biggest break in teaching came through the professional development courses offered by Jean Anastasio and Dave Perry at *APL Associates*. He credits these workshops for changing his career.

By combining the teaching strategies taught in these workshops with his own constructivist methodology, Adam was able to increase standardized test scores, get 100% classroom participation, and eliminate classroom management problems.

Of course, when Springs started their mentor teacher program, Adam jumped at the chance to help new teachers learn to become effective teachers.

After a few of years of mentoring, Adam decided to create a book on teaching strategies. **Become an Effective Teacher in Minutes: Best Teaching Practices You Can Use Now** was a direct result of his years of mentoring.

Introduction

Have you ever noticed how teachers of older students often seem to move away from using teaching strategies that are proven to work?

Why do kindergarten students have opportunities to actively engage with learning, but college students end up sitting and listening to a professor lecture for three hours?

Think about it. In which class did the students really learn more?

Unfortunately, as students progress through their education, they come in contact with more and more teachers who are focused on *managing students*, rather than on *educating students*.

Yes, of course, you are not going to get anywhere if you have no control over your classroom. But, while many new teachers think what they need are *classroom management skills*, what they really need are strong *instructional skills*.

The focus of this book is on *well-educated* students as opposed to *well-managed* students. The book is based on the premise that the best "management system" is a strong "instructional system."

I used most of the strategies described in this book in my own classroom. I also know many other teachers who implemented these strategies and we all met with the same amazing results.

Our students' grades went up (including standardized test scores), but more importantly, the students enjoyed school.

Although I taught middle school—and used these strategies with great success at that level—I trained teachers at all levels of education. I have seen the strategies in this book used effectively as early as kindergarten. In fact, I used many of them with my own son as early as four years old. And, I used these same exact strategies when I taught adults as an adjunct professor at Manatee Community College.

Remember: Information is just information unless you do something with it!

In this book you are going to learn many different strategies, methods, tips, and tricks of Effective Teachers. These are strategies and methods that inspire active learning, increase higher order thinking skills, and create life-long learners.

You will likely be familiar with some of these ideas, while others will be completely new to you.

I strongly encourage you to print this out, mark up the strategies you already use, and focus on the ones that seem most relevant to you and your teaching style.

I do not claim "originality" on all these ideas—I only originated a handful of them on my own. However, these ideas are original in their compilation and in my explanation of them.

I am a student as much as I am a teacher. I have learned from my own testing and from observing the teaching techniques of some of the best teachers I know. When applicable, I will make reference to MY teachers.

My special thanks to Dr. Barry Raebeck, Dr. Lawrence McCann, Dr. Linda Bausch, Donnelly McGovern, Lisa Seff, Ken

Goodman, and Merrill Harmin. I have learned so much from your work.

Extra special thanks to Dr. Jean Anastasio and David Perry whose professional development seminars have forever changed the way I teach. Any school district that is even slightly interested in improving their school must take a look at the professional development seminars offered by Jean and Dave at *APL Associates*.

There is so much information packed into this book that it may seem overwhelming at first, but there is a proper way to learn and apply the material taught here. It's actually very simple; don't try too many new things at once. Master two to three strategies at a time and then add two or three more. Before you know it, you will be well on your way to becoming **an Effective Teacher In Minutes**.

I hope you enjoy the book and put it to good use!!

To a wonderful career,

Adam Waxler

Chapter 1:

Strategies

It is important to note that *strategies* differ from *methods*. In Chapter 9 you will read about several proven constructivist teaching methods in which students are actively involved in constructing their own knowledge.

The strategies in this chapter are more like a series of "tricks" you can use to create an interactive classroom. Of course, there is a crossover between strategies and methods, as you will see.

I put the strategies at the beginning of the book for two reasons:

1) You will use these strategies throughout every other aspect of teaching that you will learn in this book.

2) While most of this book pertains to classroom teaching, these strategies can be used with any type of teaching. Whether you are teaching kindergarten, high school, vocational school, or graduate school— or even giving seminars in the corporate world— these strategies will increase your results.

Now on with the strategies.

TIP#1:   **Try one or two new strategies at a time. Master them, and then add one or two more. If you try them all at once, you risk doing them all incorrectly. Collaborate with colleagues so you can reflect together on what works and why.**

1. Check for understanding

(This strategy developed by <u>APL Associates</u>)

How many times have you given a list of instructions only to discover students have no idea what to do once they start the lesson?

Whether you are giving directions for a reading assignment, a worksheet, an activity, or a lab, always CHECK FOR UNDERSTANDING.

All this involves is simply asking individual students to repeat your directions. If a student can't repeat the directions, either you didn't give the directions clearly or the student was not paying attention.

In either case, call on another student. The more you call on students and CHECK FOR UNDERSTANDING, the more you will see those students paying attention and following directions.

That's right, I said "call on." It is time to start moving away from always having students raise their hands. Save hand raising for times when you are looking for volunteers.

Yes, yes, I know. Many of you just sat back and thought, "I can't just call on my students; that will increase their anxiety and inhibit them from performing at their highest level." Not so. If you have established a classroom based on *mutual* respect, kids will feel comfortable and safe (see Chapter 10: Classroom Management). To help kids feel even safer, provide them with an "out": the PASS OPTION.

2. The pass option

This is an "exit option" that *all* students have at *all* times. When a student is called on, that student can simply say "pass."

It is of the utmost importance that students understand this option and understand that "passing" is **not** a reflection on them and will not affect their grade. There are times when we all drift off and daydream—it doesn't make us bad people.

Remember: "I don't know" is a negative self-put-down. Have your students say "pass" instead!!

TIP#2: Since the PASS OPTION may be new to your students, you might want to spend some time teaching it, explaining it, and reminding them how to use it. Here are a couple of ideas:

1. Have the whole class say "pass" at the same time. They love doing this—in fact, I once had a student ask if he could "pass" from saying "pass." I thanked him for making the point, and said "yes."

2. **Post a sign.** I had a laminated sign in my room that clearly stated "Remember the Pass Option" with a cute little picture of a cartoon quarterback.

3. Wait time

After asking a question, wait at least three to five seconds before taking students' responses. I cannot stress enough the importance of this simple, easy-to-use strategy. You ask hundreds of questions a day. Whether or not you have moved away from the traditional hand raising mentioned earlier, you MUST give students time to process and retrieve information.

Yes, I know five seconds of silence may seem like an eternity in the classroom and may actually seem strange at first, but you and your students will quickly get used to this silence. The main point here is what is going on during that silence—students are thinking. And guess what? That's what we want them to do!

There are two things you will notice immediately:

1. The students who usually respond right away will have time to develop much stronger answers.

2. If you ask for volunteers, many more hands will go up as you continue to wait.

Remember: It is not a race to see who can get the answer fastest—this is not Jeopardy!!

[WAIT TIME will be addressed again in more detail in Chapter 9: Methods]

TIP#3: Try giving *yourself* WAIT TIME. When students ask *you* a question, give yourself time to process the information. Watch how much more effective your responses and follow-up questions are.

4. On-the-clock

(This strategy developed by <u>APL Associates</u>)

This is another very simple and easy-to-use strategy that will keep students on task as well as help with classroom management issues.

This falls under the category of *Specificity*. Assign a task and then set a *specific* time limit to complete that task.

Remember: Once you give a time limit—STICK TO IT!
Definite task—Definite time—Definitely stick-to-it!

TIP#4: Use a timing device! Stopwatches and egg timers help students, *and their teachers*, stick to the allotted time. You will be very impressed with how well this works and the positive impact it has on classroom management. I tell people all the time... *the most important teaching tool is a timer*.

Remember: Don't forget to CHECK FOR UNDERSTANDING!!

Here's an example:

Teacher: I want you to answer the questions on the worksheet based on the political cartoon we just discussed. You have four minutes to answer the questions. How much time do you have, Johnny?

Johnny: Four minutes (or "pass").

Teacher: What are you going to do in those four minutes, Natalia?

Natalia: We are going to answer the questions based on the political cartoon (or "pass").

Teacher: Go. (Set timer.)

Remember: If it's good, it's good to hear it a few times!!

5. The all write & the pair/share

It is important that I put in here two very simple and important strategies before we go any further. The first is the ALL WRITE strategy followed by the PAIR/SHARE.

Both of these strategies create a classroom with 100% participation, both strategies increase confidence and learning, and both strategies can and should be incorporated into all the other strategies and methods that you will learn in this book.

The ALL WRITE is, again, a very simple strategy. (You'll notice I say "very simple" a lot. I hope you're starting to see a pattern—teaching does not have to be difficult.)

In the ALL WRITE strategy, *all* your students write an answer to a question rather than respond aloud.

The reasons for this are also simple. By having *all* students write an answer to the question, you have gotten 100% of your class to respond to that question.

If they don't know the answer, have them write down the question and then the answer once it is discussed.

Here is an example from a lesson on the building of the Panama Canal from my 8th grade social studies class. (I will get into methods on how to teach later in this book. For now, you should know that the Panama Canal lesson was taught with a video clip, map work, and a short reading—**in that order**.)

The following is a simple closure question at the end of that lesson:

Teacher: Now I would like you to *ALL WRITE* down an answer to a question. There is not necessarily a right or wrong answer. It's how you back up (support) your answer. The question is based on the four different types of foreign policy that we have been discussing in this unit and based on today's lesson about the U.S. building of the Panama Canal. Here's the question: Which type of foreign policy would you argue (higher order thinking skill) the U.S. was using in building the Panama Canal?

You have three minutes to write an answer to the question. How much time do you have, Juan?

Juan: Three minutes (or "pass").

Teacher: And what am I asking you to do, Zach? (Notice: I ask the question, then name the student.)

Zach: Pass.

Teacher: What am I asking you to do, Ryan? (Notice: I did not criticize Zach. I simply went on to the next student.)

Ryan: Write down what type of foreign policy the U.S. was using when building the Panama Canal.

Teacher: Zach, what am I asking you to do? (Notice: I went back to the student that "passed.")

Zach: Write down what type of foreign policy the U.S. was using in building the Panama Canal.

Teacher: You have three minutes…Go. (Set timer)

At this point, the teacher should use the MONITOR MAP strategy, which I will discuss shortly.

First, I want to focus on what the students do when their three minutes is over—the PAIR/SHARE.

The PAIR/SHARE allows students to teach and learn from each other, and also gives the teacher time to implement the INTERACTION SEQUENCE (the next strategy).

For PAIR/SHARE, have students find partners and share their written answers with each other. Just remember to give the students a specific amount of time for sharing.

TIP#5: When using the PAIR/SHARE strategy, I sometimes tell students that they will have to tell the class what their *partner's* response was rather than their *own response* — this holds students accountable for listening to their partners.

This is how PAIR/SHARE worked in the Panama Canal lesson:

Teacher: OK, please finish up what you're writing. Partner up with the person nearest you and take two minutes to share your answers with each other.

Teacher: How much time do you have, Gabby?

Gabby: Two minutes (or "pass")

Teacher: And what am I asking you to do, Tania?

Tania: Find a partner and share our answers with each other.

Teacher: Two minutes…GO! (Set timer.)

At this point the teacher should implement the "INTERACTION SEQUENCE."

6. The interaction sequence
(picking students to respond)

(This strategy developed by APL Associates)

If you are a teacher who puts your students on task and then simply waits in the front of classroom until they are done, it's time to change.

A teacher in a student-centered classroom must always be moving around the room, and you will learn how to do this in the next strategy, MONITOR MAP.

For now, I want to focus on how you choose students to call on after a PAIR/SHARE. Keep in mind, the INTERACTION SEQUENCE has had more of an effect on building self-esteem and confidence in the classroom than any other strategy I have seen or used.

Here are the steps of the INTERACTION SEQUENCE:

- *Interview students during PAIR/SHARE*

  As you move about the classroom, quietly ask specific students what their response is to the question. That student will either give the correct answer, an incomplete answer, or the wrong answer. Either way, by the time you walk away, make sure the student knows the correct answer. You simply use a few scaffolding questions to make an incomplete answer complete or to change a wrong answer to a correct answer.

Here's an example:

Teacher: …and what am I asking you to do, Tania?

Tania: Share my answer with my partner.

Teacher: Two minutes…Go! (Teacher then approaches a pair of students and *interviews* one or both of them.) So, Sam, what do you think? What type of foreign policy was the United States using when building the Panama Canal?

Sam: I said internationalism (with hesitation in his voice).

Teacher: OK, why did you say that?

Sam: Well, we were trying to protect ourselves by making it easier for our Navy ships to get to both oceans. And we were also helping the people of Panama.

Teacher: Great, Sam. I like the way you backed up your answer. Hannah, what do you think? (Hannah is Sam's partner.)

Hannah: Well, I thought it was imperialism (now more hesitant because of the positive feedback I just gave Sam).

Teacher: OK, why?

Hannah: Well, we kinda just took the land. I mean I know Panama gave it to us, but we wouldn't have helped support their revolution to break away from Colombia if Colombia had accepted our offer to buy the strip of land (Isthmus of Panama), so it was kind of like we were being the world bully and just took the land.

Teacher: Great job of backing up your answer. Remember there is not always *one* correct answer; it depends on how you support your answer.

[Teacher then moves on to interview another student(s)]

What has this process done?

For one, it has allowed all students to compare answers with their partners, thereby allowing them to explore the topic in more depth and clarify any misunderstandings in a safe (non-anxiety producing) environment.

Secondly, it has given the teacher a great amount of insight into who has the correct answer. I now know at least two students from the example above who have correct answers and can support their answers.

Why is this second point so important? Because a teacher's job is to try to catch students being right!! (Too often, teachers ask questions for the opposite reason. Questioning should never be done as a means to embarrass students.)

Here's what you do next (in this order):

1. *Call on students you interviewed*

   First bring the class attention back to you. A simple "times up" or "stop" will suffice. (Here is where a timer is effective—when my timer went off, my students knew they needed to stop what they were doing and listen to the next set of directions). Restate the question. Then call on a student who you interviewed and knows the answer.

2. *Call on random students*

   Next, call on a student whom you did not interview.

3. *Ask for volunteers*

   This is when you ask students to raise hands.

For example:

[Timer beeps. Students stop what they are doing and listen for next set of directions.]

Teacher: The question was "Which type of foreign policy was the U.S. using during the building of the Panama Canal?" Sam? (Sam was one of the students I interviewed)

Sam: I said "internationalism."

Teacher: Why?

Sam: Because we were helping the people of Panama and also protecting our own national security.

Teacher: Great way to support your answer. How about you, Hannah? (Hannah was the other student I interviewed.)

Hannah: I disagree; I thought it was imperialism because the U.S. simply took the land. The U.S. was not really interested in helping the people of Panama if they weren't going to give us the land to build the canal on.

Teacher: Again, great way to support your answer. Jessica, what do you think? (Jessica is a "random"—not one of the students I interviewed.)

Jessica: I agree with Hannah. We offered Colombia money for the land and they refused. It wasn't until after they refused that we decided to support the revolution in Panama.

Teacher: OK, how about volunteers?

Don't forget WAIT TIME—watch in amazement as hands continue to rise!

Research shows that the example heard first is usually the one most remembered.

If you call on students you've interviewed, you can guarantee that the examples heard first will always be correct.

More importantly though, the confidence and self-esteem that this strategy builds are remarkable. I have seen this first-hand. If a student knows that they have the correct answer, they are much more likely to participate in class.

Try the INTERACTION SEQUENCE and notice how well students respond. It is an extremely satisfying feeling to see a student's self-esteem improve.

Remember: Anxiety does not produce good learning. The INTERACTION SEQUENCE greatly reduces anxiety.

Remember: A teacher's job is to catch students being right!!

Just a couple of final points on the INTERACTION SEQUENCE. The purpose of calling on random students (people you have not interviewed) is to keep all students on task—otherwise students will quickly figure out your system and will know that if they are not "interviewed" they will not have to respond. The purpose of calling on volunteers is to allow the passive learner the chance to respond.

7. The monitor map

(This strategy developed by APL Associates)

As I said before, if you are one of those teachers who sit at the front of the room waiting for your students to complete a given task, it's time to change. You need to be up and moving.

Think back to the ALL WRITE example, in which students were "all writing" the type of foreign policy they felt the U.S. was using when building the Panama Canal.

Once you put students on this task, you must go from student to student, keeping them on task and helping them with any questions. And there is a strategic method for doing this—the MONITOR MAP. While I was never a teacher who sat, or even stood, at the front of the class waiting for my students to finish a task, I did make the common mistake of going directly to the less able students first. *Yes, this is a mistake.*

There is a better order to monitor your room:

1. Go to procrastinators first.

2. Go to your less able students.

3. Anyone else.

It is extremely important to identify who the procrastinators are in each class. These are the students who say "I don't get it" as an excuse to avoid doing "it."

The trick is a quick "hit and run" tactic.

After you've put students on task, immediately go to the procrastinators and get them started. Two important things must follow:

1. Tell the procrastinator, "I'll be back in one minute (be specific); I want to see you do this..."

2. Make sure to go back to that student in that specified time.

Remember: Procrastinators are usually not your less able students; they simply put things off!!

Procrastination is planned or intentional stalling. Getting these students on task doesn't take much time; it just takes persistence. If you go to your less able students first, who require more of your time, the procrastinators will simply procrastinate longer.

By getting the procrastinators started, you can actually spend more time with the less able students. But don't forget to go back to a procrastinator in the specified time.

After you have gotten your procrastinators started, go to your less able students. And once you have gotten both the procrastinators and the less able students working, you can monitor the rest of class.

Does this sound as if you are running around the room like a chicken with its head cut off? Good, because it should.

A teacher must always be moving around the room—what is your other choice?

The goal here is to eliminate procrastination. If you follow the MONITOR MAP correctly, you will achieve this goal. Until then, make sure you have some comfortable shoes.

Here is an example:

Teacher: Based on the assembly line activity that we just completed, I would like you to complete this chart on the advantages and disadvantages of the assembly line. You have seven minutes to complete the chart on your own. Joey, how much time do you have?

Joey: Seven minutes.

Teacher: What am I asking you to do, Sarah?

Sarah: Write in advantages and disadvantages of the assembly line on the chart.

Teacher: And who are you working with, Stephany?

Stephany: By myself.

Teacher: You have seven minutes…GO!

(Having already identified procrastinators, the teacher should immediately go to them and get them on task.)

Teacher: Aidan (the token procrastinator), I want you to write advantages here and disadvantages here (actually point to chart). I'll be back in thirty seconds; I want to see at least one in each column.

(Teacher then moves on to another procrastinator.)

Teacher: Alex, I want you to write advantages here and disadvantages here (points to chart). I'll be back in thirty seconds; I want to see at least one in each column.

(Teacher then goes back to Aidan.)

Teacher: Good job, Aidan; now try and put at least two more in each column. I'll be back in two minutes.

(Teacher returns to Alex)

Teacher: Good job, Alex; now try and put at least two more in each column. I'll be back in two minutes.

(Teacher can now move on to the less able students.)

[It may seem like this took a long time, but actually it only took about one minute.]

Teacher: Amanda (less able student), I see you are having difficulty coming up with an advantage to the assembly line.

Amanda: Yeah.

Teacher: Well, let's think about the activity we just did. What is something good that came out of the assembly line?

Amanda: I don't know.

Teacher: Sure you do. Look at the stack of papers we just created with our assembly line. (Students created paper doll stick figures, with each student having one specific part to draw.)

Amanda: Oh, we were able to make a lot of them.

Teacher: That's great; write that down in the advantage column. Now try to come up with a disadvantage. Think about the quality of the paper dolls…

(Teacher can now move on to another student, and so on.)

Are you going to be able to get to every student? No, of course not, but you will have gotten to many in the allotted time, and if you have been following, you will know what is coming next…

Teacher: OK, times up. I now want you to take four minutes and share your charts with the person next you. Add anything your partner got that you did not.

And you know what comes next. Yep, that's right, the INTERACTION SEQUENCE…

Like I said, "Make sure you have a comfortable pair of shoes."

** **Important Note:** *You may have noticed a number of these strategies were developed by APL Associates. As I mentioned in the introduction, APL Associates changed my career. I would not have been the teacher I was had I not been fortunate enough to attend their workshops. For more information on APL Associates, visit their website at www.aplassociates.com.*

Chapter 2:

Time Management

I've split this chapter into two parts: *The Year* and *The Day*. I know that some of you have little or no flexibility about your schedule—you're required to teach the same lessons on the same schedule as other teachers at your grade level or on your team. If that's your situation, I encourage you to read the information about planning for the year and use what you can from it. Then focus your attention on planning daily lessons in the most effective way possible.

The Year

Planning for the *entire* year?

Yep, that's right! The *entire* year.

One of the best tips I could give both novice and veteran teachers is to plan out their entire school year.

Obviously, you will have to build in a great deal of flexibility. However, having your year planned in advance will save a tremendous amount of time during the year and ease a great deal of stress.

Most importantly though, planning out your year ahead of time allows you to focus more attention on developing different teaching strategies *during* the school year.

In essence, planning your year will make you a better teacher.

So, how does one plan out their entire year?

Don't worry, the trick is "working backwards" and designing a curriculum map.

(Visit http://thebusyeducator.com/effective to download your free sample curriculum map.)

If you are a new teacher or new to teaching in your subject area or grade level, your curriculum map will be more of a rough outline, but if you are currently teaching this subject or grade, your map should be a thorough description of your year that includes a time frame, topics, essential questions, skills, assessments, and activities.

What to do:

1. Figure out the *actual #* of teaching days (or teaching time).

2. Know your curriculum (content).

3. Divide your content into units.

4. Decide how much time to spend on each unit.

5. Create sub-units.

6. Create lesson plans for sub-units.

** Be Flexible **

Let's take these one at a time:

1. *Figure out actual teaching days*

So, how do you start? Well, as I said, you start by working backwards.

Don't start with your content; that should come next. Instead, start with the amount of time you have to teach that content—a day, a week, or a full year. But what exactly does that mean?

You need to be more specific—and realistic—about the amount of time you have to teach your material.

For example, a typical public school year is 180 days, so the assumption would be that you have 180 days to teach your content. Wrong! You are living in a dream world if you think that there are actually 180 days of teaching during that 180-day school year. There are many things that you must take into consideration such as school trips, graduation rehearsals, field days, mid-terms, final exams, retreats, school plays, fire safety day, school concerts, class pictures, job shadowing, earth day, days before vacation, etc.

And let's not forget state tests.

The 8th Grade New York State Social Studies Exam is given at the beginning of June; therefore, the twenty days of school remaining after the state test are basically shot as far as actual teaching days. Plus, the exam takes two days to administer and another two to three days to grade.

I could go on and on about the loss of teaching days. It is absolutely amazing how many days are lost.

Don't get me wrong. Many of these days are extremely worthwhile, but you need to be prepared for this loss. Don't let it sneak up and shock you. I have seen too many teachers create an enormous amount of undue stress by not preparing for the loss of teaching days.

TIP#6:   ROLL WITH IT BABY! During my first year of teaching I was so anal that any glitch in the system sent me into a tail spin. Fortunately, the teacher in the room next to mine, Adam Osterweil, took it upon himself to be my unofficial mentor. His best words of wisdom for me were, "ROLL WITH IT."

Face it. You are going to lose teaching days, and some, or even many, will be *unexpected*. All you can hope is that someone at your school (maybe even you) will take charge and create a schedule that limits the number of lost days.

So, how do you calculate *actual* teaching days?

Well, acknowledging that you are going to lose a number of days is the first step. Try as best as you can to estimate the number of days that will be missed, then add at least ten days (these are the unexpected days). Subtract that number from 180, and you will have your actual teaching days.

(# of known non-teaching days + 10, subtracted from 180 = total # of actual teaching days)

The number I came up with when teaching at Springs was 135 actual teaching days. It's scary to think we are teaching our children only 135 days out of a 365-day year, but that's a subject for another book.

2. Know your curriculum

Now that you have the number of actual teaching days, you need to know what it is you are going to teach.

First stop is your state education department. Unfortunately, this could be either a gold mine or a total bust depending on your state and even depending on the grade or subject you teach within that state.

I was very lucky; New York clearly spells out, in great detail, what is to be taught in 7th and 8th grade social studies. This is how it should be. The state tells you what the curriculum is, and it is up to you as the teacher to decide how to teach that curriculum.

So, like I said, first step, your state education department. If they don't have a curriculum, contact a department chairman at a local school district.

Once you know your curriculum, make sure everyone who teaches your grade level is on the same page.

Students should have the same curriculum experience within a school district, or there will be considerable gaps when advancing to the next grade.

What your curriculum is not!

Your curriculum is NOT your textbook. Textbooks are made by publishing companies that try to please everyone in every state and therefore squeeze way too much information into one text.

It is time to start "moving away from the textbook." In fact, in my classroom I had one set of classroom textbooks, and they stayed under students' desks. Every once in a while we would take them out to look at a picture, political cartoon, or a reading passage.

The students did not take the textbooks home. We did not follow the textbook day after day, and I didn't assign a section to read with section review questions to answer for homework each night. If you do, you are kidding yourself if you think your students are actually reading. (We'll get to reading strategies in Chapter 4: Reading)

However, let me make one point clear: I don't mean you should ignore your textbook. Just don't let the textbook drive your curriculum. If you do, not only will you fail to get through your curriculum, but you will actually be *teaching content that is not even in your curriculum*. In addition, you will hopelessly bore your students.

3. Divide your content into units

Now that you know your actual teaching days *and* know your curriculum, the fun can begin.

This is the part of teaching that I love. Designing units is where *your* curriculum takes off and you get to be creative.

To start, simply divide your units into manageable chunks that are not overwhelming to you or the kids. I divided my 8th grade curriculum into six manageable units. (It started as seven, but then reality set in).

Here is what I came up with:

Reconstruction through Present Day:

1. Reconstruction of the South

2. America Transformed (1890–1920)

   • Industrialism

   • Progressive Era

   • Foreign Policy (Spanish-American War, Panama Canal, & World War I)

3. The Roaring Twenties & the Great Depression

4. World War II

5. The Cold War

6. The Civil Rights Movement

You'll notice the title says "Reconstruction through Present Day," but I didn't actually get to the present day—that was supposed to be unit 7.

Unfortunately, there simply was not enough time. Instead of having a unit on present day issues, I made connections to contemporary issues throughout all my other units.

4. Decide how much time to spend on each unit

This part is entirely up to you and this is where your own creativity and passions come into play. This is also where you continue to "move away from the textbook."

Basically, if you "work backwards" you can figure out how many teaching days you have per unit. For the example above, I have roughly twenty-two teaching days for each unit.

[# of actual teaching days (135) divided by # of units (6) = 22.5]

However, let's say you have a passion for World War II and you want to spend more time on that part of your curriculum. Or maybe you have a creative project that is somewhat time-consuming. That's great! Just make sure you take away time from your other units.

For example, part of my curriculum covered the Progressive Era and famous people and different perspectives from that time period. The Progressive Era is traditionally a topic that holds little interest for thirteen-year-olds; nevertheless, it is a significant turning point in our history.

I decided to create a project in which students worked in pairs to conduct interviews for a television show called *Timeline*. Students pretended to go back in time to interview someone from the Progressive Era. (I will go into much more detail on this in Chapter 3: Presentations.)

The project involved creating scripts, making posters, learning lines, finding or making props and costumes, and filming the show. The entire project took time. In the end, though, the students learned about twelve different people from the time period, with a variety of historical viewpoints, and in the process, learned terms such as *laissez-faire, social Darwinism, women's suffrage*, and *muckraker*, all in an interactive and FUN way.

Of course, this took time, roughly two weeks. In fact, the Progressive Era was not even one of my major units; it was actually a sub-unit of a much larger unit, *America Transformed*, and it took up ten teaching days. That's ok though. In fact, it's great, if you are able to accomplish your objectives. I just needed to make sure I took days away from other units.

Since we spent a significant amount of time on the Civil War in 7th grade and because we ended the 8th grade year with the Civil Rights Movement, I decided to take days away from my opening unit on *Reconstruction of the South*. By shortening this unit, I could take those extra days and scatter them where I liked.

In a nutshell: Once you have determined actual teaching days and the number of units, how you determine the number of days to spend on each unit is entirely up to you…as long as you stick to the curriculum.

Remember: Be Flexible!!

5. Create sub-units

I mentioned earlier that the *Progressive Era* is actually a sub-unit of a much larger unit, *America Transformed*. Put simply, sub-units make up units (and sub-units may also be made up of smaller sub-units).

Knowing what your sub-units are will help in allocating time for each part of the year's plan. You can spend more time on one sub-unit and less time on another as long as the sum of the teaching days needed for the sub-units equals the total number of days you set aside for your unit.

Here's how it works: *America Transformed* is divided into three sub-units—*Industrialism, Progressive Era,* and *Foreign Policy*. Each sub-unit is divided into smaller sub-units or daily lesson plans. For example, the sub-unit on Foreign Policy is divided into Spanish-American War, Panama Canal, and World War I. I then created lesson plans for these topics, spending one to three days on each.

** **Important:** You should have assessments for each sub-unit. (That doesn't mean test, test, test—we will get to fair grading practices in Chapter 6: Grading.)

6. Create daily lesson plans

This is pretty self-explanatory. Once you have gotten this far and you have broken your year all the way down to individual teaching days, it is time create individual lesson plans.

Here is where you need to be flexible. In fact, you may not want to plan individual lessons more than a week in advance. Each lesson will not be perfect and you may not get through as much as you thought. That will obviously throw off your following lessons, so don't get too far ahead of yourself. The fact that you have gotten this far will already pay off in the long run.

Now, I am not going to teach you how to write a lesson plan; that is already completely overdone in most graduate schools. However, I will give you some very helpful hints that will increase learning for your students and make you a better teacher in the end.

1. Write out what you are doing every day, even if it isn't an official lesson plan. After each day, save that "lesson plan" along with any student handouts, PowerPoint slides, video clips, etc. in a folder. (You can also print out hard copies and collect them in a three-ring binder.) The extra couple of minutes this takes each day will save you countless hours in the years to come. By the end of the year, you will have a record of what you did each day along with all the handouts and visuals you need; you can then use this as your foundation for what you will do next year, making the needed adjustments and improvements along the way.

    This is GOLD! Ask me what I did on any given teaching day and I can go right to that actual lesson.

    Also, I am fully prepared to walk into an interview at any time and give a lesson on the spot.

2. Know your objectives—this is essential. If *you* don't know what the students are meant to learn from the

lesson, then how are your students going to know? The very first thing you should do is determine the objective(s) for the lesson (what your students will be able to do or know).

3. Tell your students the objectives. I can't believe I actually taught an entire year and a half without doing this, and I can't believe how many teachers still don't do this.

   At the beginning of every class, clearly tell your students what they are going to be able to do by the end of the lesson. It should not be a surprise to them. Your "objective" is what you want your students to learn, so wouldn't it be better if you clued them in on it?

   Plus, at the end of the lesson you can, and should, check to see if those objectives were met. If they were not, then something went wrong. (Yes, that will happen. It's fine as long as you figure out how to fix it).

Here's a quick example: "Today class, we are going to learn about the causes of World War II. By the end of class, you should be able to explain four major causes of the war and explain what type of foreign policy the U.S. was using at the beginning of the war."

Remember: Always CHECK FOR UNDERSTANDING!!

The Day

Well, now that you have been able to design a time management plan for the year, I have some bad news. Research shows that only about 45–50% of the teaching day is spent on teaching and learning time.

Therefore, it is extremely important to manage your time to facilitate learning. One effective strategy is ON-THE-CLOCK, which I discussed in Chapter 1.

When you give *specific* time limits, you will be better able to manage your time, and students will get more done within a given period.

Here are a few more guidelines:

1. Start and end on time

(This strategy partially developed by APL Associates)

This may seem obvious, but you'd be surprised how often teachers, professors, and people giving seminars wait for everyone to arrive.

Don't wait. Yes, I know things come up and people are late for legitimate reasons. Arriving late doesn't make someone a bad person. Starting on time is not a sign of disrespect for the person who is late, but rather a sign of respect for the people who arrived on time.

More importantly, the best time to learn is in the first and last seven minutes of a forty-five-minute class. Look at a typical forty-five-minute period:

Beginning: 1st most important instructional time (7 minutes)

Closing: 2nd most important instructional time (7 minutes)

Middle: 3rd most important instructional time (31 minutes)

Here's a scary thought: The *majority* of class time, the middle of a lesson, is the *least* effective instructional time.

Fortunately, there is a simple solution to the problem. If the beginning and ending of class are the most effective times for learning, then you simply need to create more beginnings and endings.

Take the block of time in the middle and divide it up into two or three mini-lessons, which increases the prime learning time. In other words, your teaching time should be divided into a series of mini-lessons.

Now look at the same forty-five-minute period broken up into mini-lessons:

7 minutes

10 minutes

10 minutes

10 minutes

7 minutes

TIP#7:   Using mini-lessons to create more beginnings and endings is critical to the success of a block schedule.

2. *Use timing devices*

Another effective strategy is to use time management devices such as bells, sand timers, digital timers, stop watches, etc. When you put students ON-THE-CLOCK by giving them a specific time limit, set your timer so both you and your students stick to it. While I mentioned this earlier, I felt it was important to mention it again…I simply cannot stress enough the effectiveness of a timer.

I have even seen people use different time measuring devices for different types of activities.

3. Use the "you-do-it-first" formula

(This strategy developed by APL Associates)

This is a simple formula that will most likely fade from your teaching as you get to know the age level that you are teaching and become more familiar with your content. However, it is good for new teachers and nice to fall back on if needed.

Here it is:

Whatever the task, "you do it first" and time how long it takes you to complete the task. For K–6, multiply that time by four or five minutes, and for grades 6–12, multiply that time by three or four minutes.

For example: If it takes *you* four minutes to complete a worksheet for a 6th grade science class, it is safe to assume that the average 6th grade student will need sixteen minutes to complete the same assignment.

4. Provide breaks

That's right, give your kids a break during the class. This is a hard one for many teachers to swallow. You're wondering: *How in the world can I give up time in the middle of my class for a break, when I am already under constant pressure to get through my curriculum?*

The answer is, again, "simple": You are going to give up two minutes of class time in order to get the other forty-three minutes back.

Watch how much more responsive your students are after you have given them a break (especially your afternoon classes).

Also, notice how much respect you gain from your students when they realize that you may actually understand what they are going through each day.

Chapter 3:

Presentations

How to turn dull presentations into interactivities

Remember how you dreaded student presentations when you were a kid? Hated having to stand up in front of the class while all eyes were fixated on you?

This experience was not only terrifying for you, but it was also boring for your classmates.

Doesn't bring back fond memories does it?

Of course not. So why would we put our own students through that? Just so they can share in our misery?

Here's a better idea. Turn that dull individual presentation into a group *interactivity*.

There are many different ways to do this. I'll share a few that were extremely successful in my classroom.

1. *The Interview*

The interview is a great replacement for the boring biographical presentation that all students seem forced to give at some point in their education.

In my 7th grade social studies class, as part of a sub-unit entitled *Causes of the Civil War*, we created an imaginary TV show called *Timeline* in which students go back in time to interview someone from the Civil War Era. (Obviously, this project can be done with any time period.)

Here are the basic steps:

a. Split students into pairs.

b. Provide each pair with written information on one particular person from the time period and questions to answer. (You can choose to have them search for the information themselves; just don't lose sight of time management and your objectives. Is your objective for students to be able to search for information? Maybe.)

c. Students use the information from the reading to create a script for the television show. (Scripts should include an introduction to the show, an introduction to the historical figure that says why this person is important, a ten-question dialogue between the host and the historical figure, and a closing, or wrap-up, to the show).

d. When scripts are complete, students create a poster about their person that includes a picture of the person, the person's name, and at least one thing that *visually* represents this person's position on an important event of the time (e.g., state's rights, slavery, etc.).

Note: Parts c & d can easily be switched and your students may actually write better scripts if they create their poster first.

e. Gather various props and costumes (yard sales and eBay) for the presentations and give time for rehearsing (at least one full class period).

f. Video each presentation. This can be a lot of fun, especially if you have video editing equipment.

Note: It is amazing how the props, costumes, and TV studio atmosphere increase student motivation.

TIP#8:   **What students do while they're watching the presentation is just as important as the presentation itself.**

Provide each student with a note-taking chart to fill out during the presentations.

I divided mine into three columns (name of the historical figure, most important points, and their opinion of the person).

During the presentations have students write down at least three important points about the historical figure.

After the presentations, have students PAIR/SHARE their information.

Use the INTERACTION SEQUENCE to ask questions and discuss the historical figure.

After class discussions, have the students write their opinion of the historical figure. (This could also be used as a great homework assignment: "Write your opinion of each historical figure presented today.")

Either way, by simply adding the note-taking chart and applying the INTERACTION SEQUENCE, you transformed the students' role from passive to active.

** **Important note:** the interview does not just have to pertain to historical figures. A great science teacher at Springs School, Lisa Seff, used the interview concept to teach about the planets. Instead of interviewing historical figures, the students interviewed astronauts; each *student astronaut* had just visited a different planet in our solar system.

2. *The Newscast*

The *newscast* is another great way to turn around a boring presentation. The basic concept is the same as the *interview*.

Divide your class into groups of three or four.

Give each group a different topic and information on that topic. (Again, I preferred to provide them this information rather than have them research it themselves.)

Students create a newscast on their assigned topic. The newscast includes an anchor person, an on-the-scene reporter, and a civilian. These roles can be adjusted depending on the topic and the number of people in a group.

I used the *newscast* presentation during my unit on World War II. The newscast encompassed the entire sub-unit on the U.S. home front in WWII.

Each group of students received a different American group (e.g., African-Americans, women, children, consumers) and information about the impact of WWII on that group.

Students then created their scripts and posters, collected props/costumes, and rehearsed.

Just like the interviews, I videoed the newscasts, but more importantly I made sure to have a note-taking chart for students to fill out while their classmates were presenting.

Don't forget to use the INTERACTION SEQUENCE!

3. The Skit

Skits are very similar to the *interview* and the *newscast*, but they don't necessarily require as much structure.

For example, students can be divided into several different groups, let's say six. Each group is given a different term or concept.

Each group creates a two- to three-minute skit that demonstrates the meaning of their term. They also create a poster about their term.

The students watching the skit will then have to create their *own* definition based on the skit.

Having students create their own definitions is much more effective than memorizing a definition the teacher provides.

** **Note:** *Creating posters is an important element of all these activities. The posters address various learning styles and intelligences and provide an alternative means of assessment. (Yes, include the poster in the assessment of the overall project.)*

TIP#9:   **Provide a simple rubric for you and your students to follow. Explain the rubric prior to starting any of these projects. My *interview* rubric was simply 25% for each of the following: script, poster, presentation, participation. Let pairs and groups know that grades are individual—each member of a pair or group might get a different grade.**

More on assessment in Chapter 6: Grading.

Chapter 4:

Reading

Please don't skip this chapter if you teach upper grade levels, college, or even graduate school. You might think that your students already know how to read and this does not apply to them. However, teachers can make reading much more productive at any level of education.

Think about all the reading required in an upper level college course. The professor's goal should be to have students do more than simply read; they should get the *most* out of that reading. That is the same goal teachers have at any level of education.

Fortunately, there are some very simple ways to increase reading comprehension.

First, it is important to reiterate something mentioned earlier. You have now heard me mention a few times that teachers must "move away from the textbook."

Don't misinterpret my meaning here. What I mean is this: Don't let the textbook drive your curriculum; don't use the textbook as a day-to-day guide on *what* you will teach or *how* you will teach.

Remember: You must first KNOW what your curriculum is (as we discussed in Chapter 2: Time Management) and then use your textbook as one of many supplements to support your teaching of that curriculum.

In my classes I used many different curriculum sources to teach my content, including the textbook. Each had its pluses and minuses.

Keep in mind, there is endless literature on the subject of reading. People like Frank Smith and Ken Goodman have done a superb job of researching and writing about reading, and people spend thousands of dollars on courses that teach about reading.

I am not going to say don't buy these books or take these courses; however, I can sum all of it up in two simple words: PRIOR KNOWLEDGE.

That's right, productive reading is based on what you already bring to the table when you open a text, what you already know about a particular topic, your *prior knowledge*.

Here is an example that I have heard many times in discussions about this topic:

Imagine two readers of the same age. The first reader, JoAnn, is a low level reader with a tremendous amount of knowledge on the sport of baseball (players' names, stats, history, etc.). The other student, Sarah, is a strong reader, but has zero knowledge on the sport of baseball (no interest in the sport, has never even seen a baseball game). Now, give each student a passage to read about Yankees all-star shortstop Derrick Jeter. Which reader do you think will be more interested in the topic, and which reader will comprehend more from the passage? The answer to both questions (supported by so much research you don't even want to get into it) is JoAnn.

Here is another way that the importance of *prior knowledge* was proven to me, completely by accident:

I have taken a handful of Spanish courses throughout my education. I know a handful of words and sentences, but would hardly call myself proficient in Spanish, nor could I get by in a Spanish-speaking country (unless they spoke English). I certainly couldn't read a book that was written entirely in Spanish—OR COULD I?

> During my first year of teaching I found myself completely perplexed when the school placed two new students in one of my classes a couple of months into the school year. What made the situation complicated for me (and significantly more complicated for the two students) was that neither student spoke a word of English—not a word—not even "Hello."

> I decided to dive into my closet (not to hide) to look for the Spanish version of the history textbook. I figured if I could get these students familiar with

the textbook, they would at least have some idea of what I was teaching in the class.

What I discovered next actually shocked me. With very little knowledge of the Spanish language and a great deal of knowledge of U.S. History, I was actually able to understand and comprehend the Spanish textbook.

I could actually read a book in Spanish as long as I already had significant *prior knowledge* on the subject—WOW!

Now obviously, I couldn't read every word, but reading is **not** identifying *every* word. Reading is "making sense of print." Think about it. How often do we actually read *every* word?

Here is a neat trick to try on yourself that was in Ken Goodman's book *On Reading*:

1. Read the following paragraph through once.

2. When you have finished, cover it and ask yourself the questions below.

The boat in the Basement

A woman was building a boat in her basement. When she had finished the the boot, she discovered that it was too big to go though the door. So he had to take the boat a part to get it out. She should of planned ahead.

Ok, are you sure you read *every* word?

Let's see:

1. Did you spot "boot" instead of boat?

2. Did you spot the "he" where there should have been a "she"?

3. Did you notice "a part" when it should be "apart"?

4. Did you see "through" or "though" on line four?

5. How about "should of" instead of "should have"?

6. How about the "the the"?

Don't worry if you missed many of those mistakes. That actually means you are an efficient reader. You were NOT reading *every* word; instead, you were making sense of print.

I know what you're thinking: *Great, but how do I use this knowledge to increase reading comprehension?*

Once again, the answer is simple. Increase students' prior knowledge on a subject BEFORE asking them to read about the subject.

This may be the single most important line in this entire book, so I will say it again:

YOU MUST INCREASE YOUR STUDENTS' KNOWLEDGE AND INTEREST IN A SUBJECT <u>BEFORE</u> THEY READ ABOUT THE SUBJECT!!

This is where I made the biggest and most successful adjustment to my teaching.

After teaching for two years, I was successfully using all the strategies thus far mentioned in this book, including using mini-lessons to increase the number of beginnings and endings in each class (see Chapter 2: Time Management).

But, like many teachers, I was teaching the mini-lessons in the wrong order. There is a tendency for teachers to assign reading at the beginning of the class, followed by a lab, an activity, an experiential exercise, or even a movie or video clip.

This is backwards. Students won't be interested in reading about the subject at the beginning of the class (or at least the teacher has done nothing to increase their motivation to read), and they have no *prior knowledge* on the subject, or if they do, it certainly wasn't tapped into before reading.

Once again the *simple* solution is to reverse your teaching order.

Try doing an activity or showing a video clip at the beginning of the lesson. For example, when teaching about the building of the Panama Canal (mentioned in Chapter 1), I started the lesson with an eight-minute clip from National Geographic's documentary on the Panama Canal.

TIP#10: **I didn't show the entire documentary. I wanted to increase motivation, not decrease it by boring the students to death. While you and I may love the History Channel, your students may not; therefore, I often picked short clips that increased students' motivation and held their attention.**

The clip on the Panama Canal captured students' attention, gave them a visual connection to the topic, answered some questions, and raised others. Overall, the clip increased their interest and motivation and provided them with background information (prior knowledge).

Following the video clip, I gave the students map work and questions to answer based on the map. This map work made much more sense to students now that they had a visual reference. The map work also built on their knowledge base.

The *last* part of the lesson was the reading. By that point, students were interested in the topic, had prior knowledge on the topic, and were able to understand many of the confusing terms in the reading. They were ready to read for understanding, but more importantly, they actually **wanted to read**! Give it a try and see for yourself.

Now videos are certainly not the only way to increase motivation and provide prior knowledge. This could be done with all types of activities.

Here is another example:

Nearly every social studies teacher in the country creates some type of assembly line activity when teaching Industrialism. (If you don't, you should; the kids love it.)

The problem is that most teachers have their students read about the assembly line *before* the activity. The better approach is to do the activity *first*.

The kids will experience the assembly line and will use that experience to help them comprehend the reading.

Using activities at the beginning of lessons to tap into prior knowledge doesn't just apply to social studies.

I was fortunate enough to work with arguably the best classroom science teacher anywhere. Lisa Seff has created an unbelievable passion for science at Springs Middle School and has the standardized test grades to back it up (not that I think standardized test grades are important—it's actually the passion part that is important, but hey, ever think that the two might be connected?)

Lisa is fully trained in all the strategies that are in this book. Actually, she helped me become the best teacher I could be. She has mastered this reading concept in her science classes. She performs all of her science labs and activities prior to the students reading about the various topics, and her students are the ones who benefit.

TIP#11: Don't be afraid to use music in your classroom. Music can both motivate and teach at the same time. Imagine playing Buffalo Springfield's "For What it's Worth" prior to reading about the Kent State tragedy or Bob Marley's "Catch a Fire" before reading about slavery and slave ships.

TIP#12: Don't be afraid to use picture books with older children. Picture books are great ways to increase reading motivation. Imagine the impact Dr. Seuss's *Butter Battle Book* has on teaching the Nuclear Arms Race.

Another favorite picture book author of mine is Eve Bunting. I have used Eve Bunting's books to introduce topics as sensitive as the Holocaust, Japanese Internment, and the Vietnam War. Once again, give it a try. Watch how excited older kids get for "story-time".

Now it would just not be proper to write this chapter without a few other tricks to increase reading comprehension and tap into students' prior knowledge.

One that was mentioned earlier in this book is the PAIR/ SHARE (see Chapter 1: Strategies).

I often read passages aloud to my students from various sources (including the textbook). I found that my voice inflection could emphasize and de-emphasize parts as needed. After the reading, or even during the reading, I'd stop and have students turn to a partner and share one thing that they learned or found interesting. I would then go around the room asking a few students to share what their *partners* learned.

Another great strategy that works for both read-alouds and silent reading is simply to have students ALL WRITE (see Chapter 1: Strategies) a prediction for the reading passage. You can make this as short and simple as you want, or you can extend it by having students share their predictions with their partners, then with the class, etc.

Of course, it wouldn't be a chapter on reading without mentioning the K-W-L chart. This is a fantastic tool to tap into students' prior knowledge about a topic. The chart is divided into three columns (K, W, & L).

Name: _____

Topic: _____

K What do you Know?	W What do you Want to Know?	L What did you Learn

I would give students four minutes to write what they already *Know* in the first column and what they *Wanted* to know in the middle column. It was not until they had thought about what they already knew about a topic that I would have them read.

After a certain amount of silent reading time, I had the students write what they just *Learned* in the last column.

I would then have students PAIR/SHARE and add to their last column. I usually repeated this process two times.

The KWL chart is great tool that taps into prior knowledge, but also holds students accountable for their reading.

TIP #13: Don't limit the KWL chart to just reading. Try using a KWL chart with documentaries, too.

Break up documentaries by stopping the video and having students share and add to their "L" columns every so often. Hold students accountable for watching those videos *and* increase their comprehension. Win-Win!

Chapter 5:

Homework

"My Homework Ate My Parents"
Time, Nov/Dec '99

Homework is an area in which many teachers, even veteran teachers, make the most mistakes.

Homework can be one of the most frustrating and time-consuming aspects of teaching. I have seen teachers become so frustrated with homework that they have thrown in the towel and just don't assign it anymore.

While I think throwing in the towel is wrong, I will say this: I would rather a teacher not assign homework at all, than assign it in the wrong way.

Let's get one thing straight right away: **Your class is NOT a correspondence course**. Homework should NEVER be used to teach new material.

Homework should consist of a fairly short assignment that reinforces what was done in class that day (or previous days).

I'll never forget my first student teaching experience. The class was run completely backwards. Each night for homework the students would read a section in the textbook and answer the section review questions. Besides being completely boring and unimaginative, the assigned reading was on material that had not yet been taught. The students were reading material for what was going to be taught during the next class.

If you are going to be one of those teachers that simply assigns textbook reading and questions every night, at least have the students read sections based on what they have already been taught. (Chapter 4 discussed the importance of prior knowledge on reading comprehension.)

So What Is the Right Way to Give Homework?

You need to start by understanding the *amount* of homework to give.

The purpose of homework is to reinforce and practice a concept learned in class. If you can do that with five math problems, why give twenty-five problems for homework? The students either understand the concept or they don't. The last thing you want to do is reinforce a misunderstood method or concept by making them do twenty-five problems incorrectly.

Remember: It is much more difficult to unteach something than to teach it right the first time. If students are reinforcing incorrect learning, you will be forced to unteach something.

Also, you must keep in mind the amount of time your homework will take students to complete. Don't forget the "you-do-it-first" formula (see Chapter 2: Time Management).

Let's say you gave your students twenty-five math problems for homework and each problem took two to three minutes to complete. You just gave your students fifty to seventy-five minutes of homework in their math subject alone.

Now please don't kid yourself. This will lead to one thing only: **Good Copiers**. That's right. A handful of your students will actually do the homework and the rest will copy it, which is actually better than having students reinforce the wrong concept by having them complete twenty-five math problems that they don't understand.

A good rule of thumb here is roughly ten minutes of homework per grade level for the *total* amount of homework given.

Yes, that means if you teach 8th grade, students should have no more than eighty minutes of TOTAL homework. If an 8th grade student has five subjects for homework, each subject should be roughly sixteen minutes.

And don't forget that homework should reinforce what students have already learned; it should NOT teach new material.

Homework & Time Management

One of the major problems teachers have with homework is the impact on time management.

Unfortunately, time management issues lead many teachers to make poor decisions about homework—not going over homework, not grading homework, or not even assigning homework.

- *First of all, do not assign homework if you do not intend to go over that homework in some fashion; otherwise, the students will never know if they were doing it right or not.*

  Also, if not going over homework becomes a habit, students will look at it as just "busy work," rather than something that is important.

Remember: If homework is important enough to give, it is important enough to go over.

- *Likewise, you must also grade the homework. For one, students must be held accountable for the homework. If you don't grade the homework, you will see more and more students simply stop doing it. (Wouldn't you?)*

- Lastly, if you are not giving homework at all, you are missing out on a great opportunity to increase students' comprehension of the material.

However, here is some good news: You can actually give homework, go over homework, and grade homework in a way that is not time-consuming.

The answer lies in *how* you grade the homework and how much *weight* you give homework in the student's overall grade average.

Like I said before, homework is simply reinforcing already learned material and should be a fairly short assignment. Why, then, would you make their homework grade a full 25% of their overall average? (Especially when you have no real way of controlling their homework environment—when, where, and with whom they are doing homework.)

Here is a solution: Your homework should not exceed 12–15% of the student's total average. A student's homework average should only raise or lower their overall average by a few points in either direction. Homework grades should never bump a seventy-five class average to a ninety-five. Likewise, a student with an eighty average should never fail a class because of not doing homework.

Here is another solution: When grading homework, give students one of three grades:

- √ = *full credit = 100%*
- ½ = *half credit = 50%*
- x = no credit = 0%

Simply keep a tally and then do some simple division to calculate their final homework average.

For example, if Nick did ten out of ten homework assignments and received a √ on all of them then he would receive a 100% averaged in as 12% of the overall grade.

However, if Sally only did six out of ten homework assignments and on two of them received half credit, then she would have 50% averaged in her overall grade. Note that this is only 12–15% of the overall grade; she should NOT fail the quarter because of her homework average alone.

Of course, none of this addresses how or when to discuss the previous night's homework.

I suggest having students PAIR/SHARE their homework answers at the beginning of the class. This gives students time to discuss the answers with their peers, which further reinforces the concepts and allows them to learn from each other. It also gives you time to assess their homework.

As they talk with each other, circulate, listen, and coach, using the MONITOR MAP and INTERACTION SEQUENCE. (Chapter 1: Strategies). Carry a clipboard or notebook where you can quickly write down their homework grade. (I had an individual spreadsheet for each class, and I tallied their homework total at the end of each week. At the end of the quarter, I just did a quick division problem for each student.)

Some More Homework Tips

Homework can be a very effective tool if done right. Here is a list of some helpful homework strategies that I followed every day:

- *DO NOT put homework on the board at the beginning of class. Putting homework on the board leads students to focus on getting to the homework as quickly as possible rather than on what you're doing in class. Many students will even try to do the homework in class.*

- If you must put homework on the board, wait until the end of class.

Save the last couple of minutes of class time for your students to start the homework. This is an extremely effective strategy I learned at an <u>APL</u> workshop and I was thrilled with the results. By starting the homework at the end of class, you accomplish two major goals:

1. You greatly reduce, or even eliminate, the "I didn't know we had homework" response.

2. Starting homework in class clears up any questions the students may have about how to do the homework.

For most students, the hardest part of homework is getting it started. If you use this homework strategy in your classes, you will be amazed at how much more homework gets done and how the quality of that homework improves.

- Give homework that goes "beyond the textbook."

It is ok to give reading assignments for homework (as long as the reading is about something students already learned), but use good questions that stimulate thinking.

However, don't limit yourself to just reading assignments.

Have students write journal entries or letters or draw pictures that include key terms from that day's lesson.

There are many creative homework assignments that students will actually enjoy doing and that go "beyond the textbook."

- Put your homework online.

I recommend starting a classroom blog. This way parents and students can get notified automatically each time you make a post.

(Many more assessment strategies and techniques will be discussed in Chapter 6: Grading.)

Chapter 6:

Grading

Computer Grading

Careful consideration should be given to how students are assessed in both the classroom and the district. Ideally, your entire school district is using a computerized grading system, but if not, there are still many computerized systems that you can use as an individual.

During my first year, teachers at Springs School, including myself, wasted countless hours calculating student grades on a calculator and configuring those grades within our own weighting system. I can't even begin to assess the amount of time we wasted writing grades into a grade book as well as writing out individual comments for progress reports and report cards.

Eventually, I got rid of the grade book and did everything by computer. I had over thirty comments to choose from in my comment bank. And best of all, the computer did all the calculating, even factoring in the weight I gave each category. (It's a beautiful thing).

Remember: Save, and make backups often!!

Categories & Weighting

Whether you have a computerized grading system or not, there are some things you are going to have to decide on first: *Categories* and *Weighting*.

What *categories* to create and what percentage to *weigh* each category.

My answer, as always, is keep it simple.

Here is how I set up my categories and weighting system:

- *Homework: 15% (as discussed in Chapter 5: Homework)*

- *Class participation: 15% (for many of the same reasons as homework)*

- Major grades: 70% (includes essays, tests, presentations, projects, etc.—all major grades averaged in as 70% of their total grade)

Homework was already discussed in detail in the last chapter. Class participation, however, needs some clearing up.

Class participation can be a difficult grade to establish because of its subjectivity. For me, class participation did not necessarily imply raising a hand and volunteering information all the time. In fact, if you are effectively using the INTERACTION SEQUENCE (see Chapter 1:

Strategies), there will not be all that much hand raising in your classroom anyway.

So what is class participation?

I made it clear that to participate in class, students needed to be prepared with required materials (pen/pencil, notebook, homework, etc.). Leaving these materials in their lockers was unacceptable and would lower their class participation grade.

If a student didn't have something to write with, I provided a pen or pencil. (How many times do you lose your own pen? I do all the time.) While many teachers may disagree with me on this, I have found that it is just not worth the hassle.

However, if not bringing a pen to class became a habit, that student's class participation grade was lowered.

How well a student works with others also falls in the class participation category. Students in an interactive classroom are constantly working with one another, and how well they work with others has an impact on their class participation grade.

Clearly, class participation is a subjective grade; therefore, it should never be more than 15% of the overall average.

Similar to homework, a student's class participation grade should either raise or lower a student's average by only a few points. A student should never fail a class because of a low class participation grade.

The remainder of the overall grade is made up of what I call *major grades*.

Major grades make up 70% of the students' overall average. All the major grades are put into this same category, and they include essays, projects, tests, and presentations. Yes, that means a test carries just as much weight as a project, as it should. This gives students a chance to show their abilities in various ways.

How Much Is Enough?

How many graded assignments should you give in a typical quarter?

Given that a typical quarter is ten weeks long, four to six major grades are more than sufficient. (Again, keep it simple—that's already an average of one major graded assignment every two weeks.) Any more than this could actually be detrimental to learning. Yet, every day teachers' grade books are loaded with graded assignments that conjure up time management nightmares. Many teachers feel that by giving *more* grades, each grade carries less weight and students have a better chance. There are two problems:

1 Grading time

Let's face it, teachers don't have secretaries (though we should) and most don't have teaching assistants (though we should).

By now you have probably noticed that I focus a great deal of attention on time management. It's true; I go to great lengths to reduce the amount of time spent on certain areas.

Let me make one point perfectly clear—I am not a lazy person looking for less work and an easy way out. In fact, I consistently arrived to school one to two hours before the students and before my contract said I should arrive. (Ahh…the contract—yes that too is for another book.) I also worked on weekends and during vacations. My first full days off each year (no school work at all) usually happened over Thanksgiving break.

OK, so clearly I am not a lazy person but by reducing time on task in certain areas, I was able to focus more time on the important areas—teaching methods, classroom strategies, and curriculum development.

This is the same reason I think it is crucial for a teacher to teach as few subject areas as possible. Clearly, a teacher who teaches one subject area (8th Grade Social Studies) will focus time and energy differently than a teacher who teaches four different subject areas (8th Grade Social Studies, 7th Grade Social Studies, Writing Lab, Study Skills). While both teachers may be teaching five classes per day, one has the opportunity to develop professionally by focusing on methods, curriculum, and lesson planning, while the other merely survives.

2. Less is more!!

If students have too much work, they are forced to "just get it done". But do we want to create a generation of people whose goal is to "just get it done"?

No, of course not. We want students to dig deeper and explore concepts, question things they don't understand, and pursue the answer. If working on an assignment triggers an interest in something, they should feel free to pursue that interest, not put it off because there is just not enough time.

For example, I once had an education professor who assigned so much work that it was simply *overload*. It became, as my own students would say, "busy work." Sure, I could get it all done, but the more assignments I did, the less I got out of each one.

It's really simple when you think about it: If I have x number of hours set aside for graduate work and in that time I can do either five assignments or fifteen—which assignments will I get more out of?

Fair Grading

What is "fair" when it comes to grading?

Well, first of all, four to six major assignments per ten-week quarter is fair. But remember, not every student excels at the same type of assessment. A student, who does well on a test or an essay, may not necessarily do well on a project and vice-versa.

Therefore, it is important to mix up the assessments. Let's say you have six grades. In that case try two tests, two essays (one formal, one creative), and two projects.

As for "fair" testing, give the students plenty of time on tests. I used short answers mostly. It is important for students to be able to put answers in their own words. These short-answer tests included a mix of key terms, political cartoons, graphs, reading passages, and a short essay.

I did include a few multiple-choice questions on every test so students were familiar with those types of questions. I also made sure to teach students strategies, or "tricks," for answering multiple-choice questions because they were bombarded with multiple-choice questions during state testing.

"Fair" Grading No-No's

While we are on the subject of "fair" grading practices, I need to mention two of the big "no-no's" —things many teachers do, but should not:

1. *Dropping the lowest grade*

While I understand the "everyone has a bad day" reasoning behind dropping the lowest grade of the quarter, there are just too many problems with this.

First of all, your grading system should not be a surprise to your students, so if you have a policy of dropping the lowest grade you must tell your students. Then the question becomes "Are students who are satisfied with their grade going to be expected to perform on the last assignment of the quarter?"

What if your last assignment is a group project and one student can afford to get a zero because he knows it will be dropped? Don't think this happens? Think again. I ran into this problem my first year teaching when I still dropped students' lowest grades. That was the first, last, and only year I dropped grades. The problem is that dropping grades limits your ability to hold students accountable.

2. *Extra credit*

That's right, extra credit, and even make-up tests, are a big "No-No."

The only thing extra credit reinforces is "No Responsibility."

Students must take responsibility for their actions. If students know they can take a make-up test, they might think there is no need to study for the test the first time around. They can simply take the test again if they do poorly.

Plus, what about the students who studied hard? It is hardly "fair" that those who did *not* work hard are given more chances. What does that teach our children anyway?

This goes true for extra credit as well. I sometimes had students ask me, "If I have a poor homework grade, can I have some extra credit work to raise my average?" My answer was always "no."

If I gave extra credit work to a student who had refused to do homework for eight weeks, I was reinforcing that it is ok not to do homework, that there is a way out. When that same student asked, "Well then what can I do?" I responded with, "The homework, when it's due."

I was not trying to be mean. I was actually being "fair," and more importantly, I was being CONSISTENT!

However, I allowed a slight exception. I gave students an opportunity to earn bonus points. The big difference between this and other types of extra credit is that bonus points are offered prior to tests and are used to help students study for the tests.

I called this the *Ticket-to-the-Test*. Before every test, I gave the students an opportunity to earn three to five bonus points on the test by creating their own test with a minimum of ten questions and answers.

They could create the test in any format they wanted, but they had to hand in their Ticket-to-the-Test prior to taking the real test.

This forced students to anticipate possible questions and reinforced the terms and concepts that would be on the test.

Since students received bonus points, I made this an optional assignment. Those students who did the extra work benefited doubly; they got three to five extra points, but they also were studying, so their actual test grade went up as well.

My kids really loved this one and told me all the time how much it helped them study.

Chapter 7:

Review Games

"If it is not fun a fair part of the time, it's probably no good, and definitely won't last."

Barry Raebeck

Want to know how important review is?

Here is a little bit of information I learned at an APL workshop that may lead to some insight on why students look at you with blank stares when you ask them a question about a previous day's material:

The Learning Curve (or rather, the Forgetting Curve)

- *20 minutes after teaching, 45% is lost*

- *60 minutes after teaching, 55% is lost*

- 24 hours after teaching, 65–75% is lost

Studies on memory loss show that teachers need to review and reinforce in every lesson. (Chapter 8 will discuss an effective review strategy that every teacher should use every day.)

This chapter will focus on the proper way to use review games (and not just the same old *Jeopardy*).

I am going to take you through a step-by-step process of five of my favorite review games that can be adapted to any subject area at any level.

All of these review games have similar characteristics:

- *Students work in small groups.*

- *They have time to review material with group members.*

- *How well the group does depends on the entire group.*

- *All students are involved in the game.*

- Students are having fun!!

1. Poker Review

This is a game I developed using a teaching strategy that actually failed miserably. Fortunately, I was able to turn that failure into one of my most successful review games.

- *Divide students into mixed ability groups of four (five if necessary)*

- *Allow students ten minutes to study their review sheets, making it clear that how well the group does in the game depends on all members of the group knowing the terms on the sheet. Also, let them know that they will not be allowed to discuss the answers once the game has begun, so "now" is their discussion time.*

- Hand each group a *Lettered-Heads* sheet—at the top of the paper are the letters *A* through *D* (or E if there are groups of five) with lines next to each letter. Below that are the numbers 1 through 10, with space to write answers next to each number. Have each student in a group write their name next to a letter.

Explain the rules:

a. Teacher asks a question followed by a letter (question then letter).

b. The student whose name is next to that letter writes the answer next to the appropriate number for that question.

c. If the student gets the answer right, the group gets a playing card.

d. If the student gets the answer wrong, no playing card.

e. At the end of ten questions, each group makes the best poker hand possible with their cards and groups compare hands to see who wins.

Here are some helpful hints:

- *Put poker rules on the board (order of poker hands— four of a kind, straight flush, etc.)*

- *Remind students that they can't discuss answers. (The quiet during this review game is an added bonus.)*

- Have a student from each group pick a wild card. It's just more fun that way.

You can usually squeeze a ten-minute review plus two poker games into one forty-five-minute class.

2. Catch Phrase

This is probably the students' favorite game. It is exciting, fast-paced, and fun.

I usually used this game for a shorter review, which can help contain the sometimes noisy excitement. It works great on those days when you lose part of a class period for some reason.

Here are the steps:

- *Prior to the game, create cards containing important terms from your current unit, one term per card. (Eventually you will have created cards for all of your units and will be able to do this game on a moment's notice).*

- *Divide the class in half—give review time if necessary.*

- *Call up one person from each team to be a responder. These students sit at a table or desk in the front of the room, facing their teammates.*

- *Explain the rules:*

- *Teacher will start a timer. (Use a timer that beeps— this adds to the excitement.)*

- *Teacher places a card in front of one of the responders, who then gives verbal clues to get their team to guess the word on the card. The responder can't use any part of the word or say "it sounds like..." or "it starts with...." (If the responder breaks any of these rules, their team loses that round.)*

- *If the team gives the correct answer, the teacher then places the next card (new term) in front of the other responder. That student then tries to get their team to guess the new word. (If the first team answers incorrectly, the second team gets a chance to guess the word before getting a new word.)*

- *If the second team guesses correctly on the new word, a new card goes back to the first responder and so on.*

- *This back and forth process goes on until the timer buzzes (approximately one minute).*

- *Whichever team is currently trying to guess when the timer goes off loses that round. The other team automatically gets one point and has a chance to guess the word. If they're successful, they get an additional point.*

- After each round, call up new responders from each team.

Here are some helpful hints:

- *Don't play beyond ten points per game, or things just get hectic.*

- *Don't be afraid to try this game because of the noise potential! It may be the most fun you see students have during school.*

3. Memory (Concentration)

As far as actual reviewing is concerned, this may be the game in which students learn the most.

The game is based on the same concept as the memory (concentration) card game that almost every student is familiar with.

- *Prior to the game, create two identical sets of cards with important terms from your current unit, one term per card. A quick way to do this is to divide 8 ½" x 11" sheets of construction paper or card stock in half and write the term in each half. (Eventually you will have created cards for all of your units and will be able to play this game on a moment's notice.)*

- *Divide your students into mixed ability groups of four (five if necessary).*

- *Allow students ten minutes to study and review, making it clear that how well the group does in the game depends on all members of the group knowing the key terms from the unit. Also, let them know that they will not be allowed to discuss the answer with group members in this game, so "now" is their discussion time.*

- While students are studying their terms, pick two sets of ten terms (twenty cards) and lay them on the floor face down in one pile so the students can't see the terms. Remember to mix the cards.

Explain the rules:

One person from the first group comes up to the game, flips over the top card, and gives the definition for the term on the card (or answers a teacher's question about the term).

If the answer is correct, the student can then try to find the matching term. (It is unlikely that students will find matches right away since they don't know where the terms are, but that is a good thing as you will see.)

If the student finds the match, that student gets to go again.

If the student does not find the match, or gets the answer wrong in the first place, the student simply turns the cards back over and a student from the next group gets to "Come on down."

Here's the catch: The winning group is the group that takes the last pair off, not the group who took off the most sets. (This is important because this is how you will keep all groups involved in the game right up until the very end.)

TIP#14: There are many times a student will not know a particular term and is forced to flip the card back over. However, it is likely that that term will be flipped over several more times with the *correct* definition, but *no match*. This allows all the students to hear terms over and over again in a fun and exciting way.

It is important that students state the definition (or answer) no matter how many times that card has already been seen. The repetition of terms and definitions is what makes this game so successful.

4. *Basketball Review*

To make this game as fun as can be, I suggest shopping around at your local yard sales or on eBay to find a *Little Tikes* basketball hoop and ball.

We bought ours at a yard sale for $3.00. However, you can order a new one through amazon.com for $35.00.

You could also use other materials to simulate a basketball game, such as a bucket and a tennis ball.

Again, this is another great game that will have the students laughing and enjoying school, while at the same time actually learning in a constructive environment.

The game starts like the others:

- *Divide students into mixed ability groups of four (five if necessary).*

- Allow students ten minutes to study and review, making it clear that how well the group does in the game depends on all members of the group knowing the terms from the unit.

Explain the rules:

The teacher asks a question and students have five seconds to discuss the answer with others in their group.

The teacher calls on a student in the first group to answer the question (no hand raising). If the student gets the answer right, the group gets five points and a chance to shoot a basket for one extra point. (Sometimes I even gave them two or three extra points.)

If the answer is wrong, the teacher immediately calls on a student from group 2.

If group 2 answers correctly, they get three points for the *steal* and a chance for one extra point by making a basket.

Once the question is answered correctly, ask a new question, beginning with a student from group 2. If they answer correctly, the group gets five points and a chance to shoot a basket for one more point.

Continue the process making sure to stop with enough time for one final question where the students get to bet their points. (This keeps all the students involved right up to the very end.)

For the final question, each group decides how many of their total points they want to bet and writes the bet on top of a piece of paper (without letting other groups know).

Once all bets are in, the teacher asks the final question. Groups have two to three minutes to answer the question and write the answer on the paper.

When time is up, the teacher collects the papers and tallies their totals on the board. The winner is the group with the most points.

5. *Ring Toss Game*

This game is similar to the basketball game. You will need a ring toss set, which you might be able to borrow from your school's Physical Education department or buy at a yard sale.

Most ring toss sets have five poles. Poles are usually labeled with point values but if not, label them yourself.

Give each team three rings. A student who gets the correct answer throws all three rings and adds up the point total.

The teacher then gives the option of either adding points to the team's score or taking away points from another team's score. This adds a little excitement and a lot of fun!!

(Since the points vary, there is no "steal" in this game.)

Final Thoughts on Review Games

Review games are a tremendous amount of fun. In my classes we always played a review game before a test.

If done correctly, review games are not only fun, but they are also great cooperative learning tools. Too often, teachers play review games where one student plays and the rest of the class sits idly watching. The games in this chapter keep *all* the students involved throughout the *entire* game.

TIP#15: Review is crucial to student learning. Review games don't have to be played just before tests. You could also play games to break up lessons and review material from past units; the students will appreciate it and respect you for it.

TIP#16: I tended to stay away from giving bonus points for prizes during review games only because it takes away from the *Ticket-to-the-Test* (see Chapter 6: Grading). Instead, I gave winning groups candy, or sometimes I handed out random prizes.

Chapter 8:

Room Layout

The classroom is where the magic happens; how your room is arranged has a huge impact on teaching and learning (assuming you have your own room). While you might think your space offers little flexibility, there *are* factors you can manage. The key is to set up your space to match your teaching style.

In this chapter, I will explain how and why I planned my room the way I did—and it was specifically connected to how I taught my class.

Seating

I will tell you right from the start, I did *not* assign seats to my students.

Why? I wanted students to feel comfortable. Think about it. When *you* take a class don't *you* want to choose where you sit?

I know what you are thinking…classroom management nightmare. Not so. We will get to classroom management in Chapter 10 but believe me, it's not as difficult as people make it seem.

I am not criticizing teachers who assign seats. In fact, most teachers I know *do* assign seats. But I never did, and never had a problem.

If you *are* assigning seats, I do make one strong suggestion: Please rotate your assigned seats every couple of weeks to give students a chance to sit with and work with a range of classmates.

Actually, the real reason I didn't assign seats is that it would have been too difficult with the layout of my classroom and would not have fit with my teaching style.

My seats were rarely in the same place two days in a row, so the students would have been completely confused.

Every morning I quickly arranged the desks to meet the needs of the lesson. The desks were set up in pairs, threes, groups of four or five, or even divided in half. It all depended on what we were doing that day.

For example, if we were playing one of the review games mentioned in the previous chapter, the desks would already be set up in groups of four when the students arrived. This saved a tremendous amount of time and actually reduced classroom management problems. Once the students were seated, I could easily and quickly move them into new groups if I thought it was necessary. (Most times where they were sitting was just fine—they enjoyed the class more if they sat with whom they wanted.)

Of course this doesn't just go for review games. If you are following the strategies laid forth in this book, then you have created an interactive classroom, with a high degree of group work and interaction between students. Having students sit in evenly spread out rows will only inhibit this interaction.

Don't let your seating arrangement guide your teaching. Think about what strategies you plan on using most and design a seating arrangement around those strategies.

Remember: Don't let classroom management dictate your class!!

TIP#17: **If you are starting to apply the ideas of this book by adding a couple of simple strategies such as PAIR/SHARE, or even the INTERACTION SEQUENCE, and are worried about moving away from assigned seating and rearranging your desks too much, there is a simple solution. Let's say you have six rows of desks; instead of having them evenly spaced out, move the two rows on both ends slightly closer together and the two rows in the middle slightly closer together. This creates three rows of pairs, rather than six single rows, giving students natural partners to pair and share ideas.**

The Walls

Believe it or not, there is a method to the madness of what should go up on each wall in your classroom.

Too often teachers put things up all over the place, but too much on the walls can actually be distracting.

If you are going to display every students' work after a project, I would suggest taking the display down after one week and then moving a few favorites to a wall reserved for student work.

Back Wall

Use the back wall to your advantage. This is another fantastic tip I learned from an APL workshop and it works great!

Think about it. Which person in the classroom looks at the back wall the most? That's right, the teacher—even teachers who move around the classroom a lot. So use the back wall to your advantage.

The back wall is where you should put up *your* goals that *you* want to work on as teacher.

For example, I was fortunate to have a dry-erase board on my back wall and used the board to list strategies that I didn't want to forget to use such as ON-THE-CLOCK, MONITOR MAP, INTERACTION SEQUENCE, etc.

You'll be amazed out how much this helps, especially when beginning to use these strategies. Write the one or two strategies you want to try first, then add two more, and so on.

The back wall is also good for other things you don't want to forget.

I posted our schedule on the back wall so I could easily refer to specific times. Also, I had reminders for myself. For example, as the 8th grade advisor I co-ran the 8th grade trip, 8th grade graduation, and the video project. There were fundraisers, monies due, and meetings happening all the time for these projects. It was much easier for me to remember to remind students about these times if the information was staring me right in the face.

Side Wall(s)

I'll keep this simple. The side walls are where I put my examples of student work and other various things such as inspirational quotes. These items should <u>not</u> be on the front wall.

Front Wall

The front wall is saved for things that benefit the students educationally.

The front wall goes along with my theory that *less is more*. If the front of the room (where the students focus the majority of their attention) is *less* cluttered, things will make *more* sense to the students.

Remember: You want your front wall organized and easy to understand. This will make learning easier for the students. Plus, you never know when an administrator will walk in. It would be nice for the Principal to look at your front wall and be able to tell exactly what it is you are doing.

The front wall in my classroom had one rule clearly posted front and center. Notice I didn't say *rules*. We had one rule: "Respect People, Respect Property" (we will get into rules in Chapter 10: Classroom Management).

My bulletin board was also in the front of the room. On it was clearly posted the name of the unit we were currently studying, pictures and primary sources that represented the unit, and a couple of essential questions for that particular unit. (Notice, this is not where I put student work.)

TIP#18:   The front board is reserved for the three things every teacher must have every day!! The *Do Now*, the *Agenda*, and the *Objective*!!

If you want to see students' achievement skyrocket, you MUST post these three things on your front board!!

1. The "Do Now" Questions

Do Now is a critical piece of your classroom. It consists of one to four questions that you write on the board each day before students arrive. Students must write answers to the questions as soon as they get to class. These questions provide an important daily review, and greatly reduce classroom management issues.

Depending on the age of the students, have them either write their answers in a complete sentence or write both the question and the answer.

I also instructed students to keep an ongoing list of their *Do Now* questions and answers. These made great review guides for tests, especially mid-terms and finals.

Remember: Research shows that it takes 2000 correct repetitions to master something!!
The Do Now provides practice of previous skills; you will see performance scores skyrocket!!

TIP#19: As often as possible, your *Do Now* should be three questions: something old, something from the not so distant past, and something recent. This helps to keep old stuff from fading too much.

TIP#20: Your objectives from the day before make excellent *Do Now* questions. (See *Objectives* below)

TIP#21: Take attendance and even check homework while students are doing the *Do Now.*

2. The Agenda

In the upper right hand corner of your front board you should neatly write what you are doing in class that day. This is your *Agenda.*

Your class should not be a surprise to your students. Let them know what it is you are going to do that day. And, don't just write it, tell them.

I wrote the date and below that a brief outline or list of what we were going to do.

For example:

<u>Today: 11/05/06</u>

o Review Foreign Policy

o Spanish-American War

- *Examine newspaper headline*

- *Song: "Editor's to Blame"*

- Text reading

I then boxed this in to keep it neat and separate from the *Objective* and the *Do Now*.

The Agenda is basically a version of the day that the students can easily understand.

The next step is to actually go through and explain it to them. I did this after the students had completed the *Do Now*.

For example:

> "Today we are going to start off with some review, something from the beginning of the year, something from a month ago, and then something from yesterday's class (point to *Do Now* questions as your examples). After the *Do Now* we will continue this part of the unit on foreign policy by taking a close look at the Spanish-American War. I have an actual newspaper from 1898 that we are going to examine, a song from the time period that we are going to listen to, and then a short reading passage from the

textbook..." (Notice the reading came at the end of the lesson.)

You would naturally follow this introduction to the class by clearly stating the *Objectives*.

3. The Objectives

The *Objectives* are the single most important part of your lesson.

Both you and your students MUST know what the objectives are of any lesson. I can not stress the importance of this enough. This is what the whole class is about, this is the whole purpose of your lesson, this is what your "students will be able to do" by the end of the class.

TELL YOUR STUDENTS THE OBJECTIVE—it shouldn't be a surprise.

Now that I've made that perfectly clear, let me explain what I did. Directly under the *Agenda*, in its own neat little box in the *lower* right hand corner of the board I clearly stated the objectives.

For example:

Objectives

- *Define: Yellow Journalism*

- *Explain at least 1 cause and 1 effect of the Spanish-American War*

- Argue which type of foreign policy the U.S. was using during the Spanish-American War

(Notice that the objectives went from lower order to higher order thinking skills—this is a good idea whenever possible).

Immediately after telling the students the *Agenda*, I then went on to explain the *Objectives*.

For example:

"…what you are going to be able to do by the end of class today is define "Yellow Journalism," explain at least one cause and one effect of the Spanish-American War, and all of you will be able to make an argument as to which type of foreign policy you think the U.S. was using and why you think that…"

Here is a good chance to quickly CHECK FOR UNDERSTANDING (see Chapter 1: Strategies).

And, don't forget to make sure your students can do those things at the end of class (see Chapter 11: Closure).

TIP #22: Use different colors to box in your *Do Now*, *Agenda*, & *Objectives*—this will keep them separated and give them added importance. (A student told me to do this one day, and I thought it was a great idea.)

TIP #23: Please don't put the teacher's desk front and center. Those days are long over.

Final Thoughts on Room Layout

As you can see, there is much more to designing the layout of your room than you might originally think.

Remember: Your room layout should reflect how you teach!!
Don't let classroom management dictate your room layout!!

Chapter 9:

Methods

Pros & Cons of Constructivism

As you may have guessed, my philosophy of education is heavily based on constructivist theories such as those of Piaget and Vygotsky.

Simply put, constructivists believe that humans learn best when they are actively involved in constructing their own knowledge.

This means we educators need to move away from teacher-centered classrooms in which the teacher basically gives information for the students to memorize. It is significantly more effective for a student to create their own definition of a key term, using context clues, than to get the definition from the teacher.

However, there are a couple of things to keep in mind when using constructivist methods.

First of all, constructivist methods are time-consuming.

Secondly, they are based in theory, created in what I like to call the "perfect world," where students come in prepared and eager to learn, leaving all their problems outside the classroom, and everyone helps each other out of the goodness of their heart.

The problem is I didn't teach in the perfect world; I taught in *middle school*.

Because so few teachers get the chance to teach in this "perfect world," many teachers throw up their hands and say that these constructivist methods are simply unrealistic.

I beg to differ.

I put this chapter on constructivist methods towards the end of this book because it builds on what you've learned so far. If you are applying the teaching strategies of this book, particularly Chapter 1: Strategies and Chapter 2: Time Management, you can use constructivist methods with any age group (even middle school).

In fact, you will be amazed at how well constructivist methods work when used in conjunction with the rest of this book.

You will also be thrilled at what I call the "light bulb" phenomenon. This is when you can see the light bulbs going off in students' heads as they actually construct their own meaning of sophisticated terms.

In this chapter I include the four constructivist methods that I used most often in my own class.

1. Pattern Search

A pattern search is basically using several examples (and non-examples if necessary) of a particular concept in an attempt to have students create their own definition of that concept.

TIP#24: **Have students create a definition on their own first, then stick a term to it.**

A pattern search has several easy steps to follow:

- *Start by showing an example of your concept.*

- *Ask students to observe and describe what they see. Make sure students stick to what they can see, not what they can infer. (This is a good place to have students PAIR/SHARE what they see or ALL WRITE what they see. That is what I mean by incorporating the strategies from Chapter 1 into the constructivist methods in this chapter.)*

- *Show a second example of your concept.*

- *Ask students to observe and describe what they see.*

- *Repeat with a third example. (Always use a least three examples and make sure students don't call things out. Some students will get it after just two or even one example.)*

- *Now you have the option of throwing in a non-example. (This works to make the characteristics of the examples stand out more.)*

- *Have students compare the examples.*

- *Prompt the students to identify characteristics and patterns in the examples.*

- *Have students explicitly state the patterns in a definition by writing a sentence describing the concept.*

- Apply their definition to additional examples and non-examples.

Remember: You do NOT have to tell students the name of the concept. Wait until they come up with the definition, and then give their definition a name.

Here is an example of how I used the pattern search method to get 8th grade students to define "propaganda."

a. I started by holding up a WWI army recruiting poster that was designed to appeal to a person's sense of pride. I asked the students to ALL WRITE what they saw in the poster (I told them to stick to only what they could see, not what they could infer).

b. I then had students PAIR/SHARE their observations and used the INTERACTION SEQUENCE to call on students to hear their responses.

c. I then repeated the same process using a present-day television Marine recruiting commercial that was designed to appeal to a person's sense of adventure.

d. For my third example, I played the 1917 army recruiting song "Over There," a song clearly designed to get men to join the army by appealing to their emotions.

e. After students had observed the characteristics and shared their information with partners, I had them identify patterns that existed in all three examples.

f. As students began to identify patterns, I put their information on the board.

g. I then had students ALL WRITE their own definition. (I never told them that they were writing a definition for the term *propaganda*.)

h. I then had the students PAIR/SHARE their definitions while I used the INTERACTION SEQUENCE to determine who I would call on.

i. The definition that the students created themselves went something like this (words in parentheses are mine): "All the examples were different forms of advertising (communication) designed to get you to join the Army (influence your opinions or actions) by appealing to your emotions."

I kid you not, that was what they came up with.

Those thirteen-year-old kids were actively involved in constructing their own definition of a sophisticated concept.

j. Once we had a good working definition, I told the students that the term they just defined was *Propaganda*.

2. Socratic Questioning

Teachers ask a tremendous number of questions. Some estimates are as high as 500–800 questions per day.

Questioning must be a part of how you teach and should be incorporated into every strategy you use as a teacher.

However, teachers often just throw around questions in a haphazard manner or give immediate responses to students' questions without any real thought involved.

Instead, teachers should use a method called "Socratic Questioning."

Here are the proper steps in Socratic Questioning:

- *Design key questions*

  Always go from broad to narrow. In the *Pattern Search* above, students were first asked what they can see in the picture. This is a very general, or broad, question that has many possible answers.

- *Students internalize the question*

  The students PAIR/SHARE the question and their answers.

- *Foster responses*

  The teacher should nurture responses while using the INTERACTION SEQUENCE.

  How a teacher fosters responses from students is a critical step in the Socratic Questioning process.

Here is a simple strategy. Just remember Q-SPACE:

Question

Start with broad, general questions.

Silent waiting time

Wait five seconds before you call on a student so all students have a chance to think through the answer.

Wait another five seconds to respond to your students' responses so you, the teacher, have time to internalize their answers and give a valid response yourself.

Probing

After giving yourself WAIT TIME, you will be better able to ask follow-up or probing questions. Now is the time to move to more narrow questions that will dig a little deeper.

Accepting

Do NOT just repeat your student's answer (a bad habit that we all fall in to).

Instead, follow the above steps, then accept the answer and move on.

However, DO NOT accept incorrect answers (another bad habit).

Clarifying & Correcting

After using probing questions, make sure you clarify any misconceptions and correct any wrong answers.

Elaborating & Extending

Ask more narrow questions to get students to expand on their answers: "Why did you say that, Johnny? What did you see in this picture that made you think that?"

Ask other classmates to help expand on answers: "Can you add something to her answer, Alejandro?" (Remember, you have already "interviewed" them during the INTERACTION SEQUENCE.)

TIP#25:   **Many teachers are against correcting wrong answers for fear that they will hurt the student or lower self-esteem. This is wrong.**

You are the teacher, and accepting wrong answers will only confuse students. Yes, many teachers will instead tell the student that the wrong answer was actually an answer to "such and such," but that can also be confusing so be careful with that one.

The best thing to do is use the INTERACTION SEQUENCE. That way you can do your correcting while you are "interviewing" various students rather than having to correct a student in front of the whole class.

Either way, it is very important that you correct wrong answers. You do not want students to reinforce incorrect learning.

Remember: It is extremely difficult to unteach something!!

3. Rationale Inquiry Method

In order to understand the Rationale Inquiry Method, we must first understand the basic concept behind a teacher demonstration.

A demonstration *is* a teacher-centered activity.

The teacher is doing and telling while the students are listening and watching. The students are not involved in constructing their own meaning around anything.

There are many good reasons to use a teacher-centered demonstration, such as motivating students and managing time.

Remember: Student-centered activities are definitely more time-consuming.

You have to know when and where to directly teach your students and when to allow them to construct their own understanding.

That is why it is crucial to know your objectives. If your objective is to have your students learn to create a graphic organizer on their own, then they should do just that.

However, if your objective is for your students to explain five causes of Industrial Growth and they happen to be writing those causes in a graphic organizer, then save yourself the time and just give them the graphic organizer with the causes written in.

Likewise, if your objective is to motivate students at the beginning of class, a teacher-centered demonstration is a great idea.

However, if your objective is for students to construct meaning from the demonstration, then you want to use the Rationale Inquiry Method.

The Rationale Inquiry Method is simply a combination of a *Demonstration* and *Socratic Questioning*. Basically, it is a demonstration with a series of good questions to help students develop the rationale for the concept.

For example, most science teachers are familiar with the "egg in the bottle" trick. The teacher takes a hard boiled egg (peeled) and an empty two-liter plastic bottle with an opening slightly smaller than the egg. The teacher then lights a piece of paper on fire, puts the burning paper into the bottle, places the egg over the opening, and everyone watches in amazement as the egg gets "sucked" into the bottle without breaking.

This is a great demonstration that holds the students' interest and motivates them to learn how this happened. It is a very effective, time-efficient demonstration that can be used to introduce the concept of "pressure."

However, the teacher could change this from a *demonstration method* to a *rationale inquiry method* in which the students develop their own definition of the concept of *pressure*. This is done by adding Socratic Questioning throughout the demonstration.

Each time a new step is added to the demonstration the teacher can use Q-SPACE (mentioned earlier) to allow the students to form their own definitions.

Remember, start with broad questions than move to more narrow questions and don't forget to use the INTERACTION SEQUENCE.

By the end of the demonstration, through teacher questioning, the students will have constructed the knowledge that the air was burned up inside the bottle and that the egg wasn't actually *sucked* into the bottle, but rather, the outside pressure *pushed* the egg into the bottle.

4. *The Cooperative Jigsaw*

The Cooperative Jigsaw is a fantastic method that, if done correctly, has tremendous results. I used this strategy often in my own classroom.

However, you should be warned, it can be time-consuming.

It's very simple to do and can be used for any subject at any level of education. In fact, the Jigsaw is a great way to turn a dull lesson that struggles to capture students' attention into a lesson where EVERY student is actively involved.

Here's how it works:

1. Decide how many things you are teaching (e.g., five causes of Industrial Growth).

2. Divide students into the number of groups equal to the number of things you are teaching. For example, when I taught the five causes of Industrial Growth, I split the students into five groups. (Of course, my room layout was already set up in five groups when the students came into the room—ahh…how I love to save time!!)

3. Each group then has a specific time limit to become an expert on one thing. For example, each group received information on one of the five causes of Industrial Growth, and each group became an expert on their particular cause.

TIP#26: I found it critical to give the students something to do in their "expert" groups rather than just telling them to read the information.

For example, in each "expert" group, students not only received information on their cause of Industrial Growth, but they also received a graphic organizer, or chart, with five blank areas to be completed. Students worked within their expert groups and wrote in important information for their particular cause.

4. Once students have become "experts," it is time for them to teach their expertise to a new group. Take one person from each "expert" group and place them into new groups. Assigning numbers is a quick and easy way to do this—assign one person in each group #1, one person in each group #2, and so on.

Then tell 1's, 2's etc. where to gather.

5. Once students are in their new groups, each student will have a certain amount of time to teach the other group members about their area of expertise.

TIP#27: The chart, or organizer, that the students completed in their "expert" groups can now be used in the new groups. Students must complete their charts based on the information that the new group members provide.

TIP#28: I found it very helpful to give students a specific order for who will go first, second, etc. This saved time and prevented procrastination.

6. When all is said and done, students will have completed charts on a particular topic, and every student in the class will have been involved.

TIP#29: I often allowed students to use their completed jigsaw charts on a test. This helped motivate all the students to do their best. If you do decide to do this, just make sure you tell the students beforehand.

Final Thoughts

Constructivist methods *are* time-consuming. The Cooperative Jigsaw on the Five Causes of Industrial Growth took an entire class period. I certainly could have given the students a list of the causes and gone over them in just a few minutes, but the students would not have retained the information, they would not have constructed their own meaning, and worst of all, they would have been BORED!

It is critical that you know your objectives and stick to your plan. In doing so, you will be able to decide when it is appropriate to use these constructivist methods and when you must use a more teacher-centered approach.

Remember: Most of us don't get to teach in the "perfect world." I taught middle school.

Chapter 10:

Classroom Management

Many teachers would argue that classroom management should be the first chapter in any book about teaching because without being able to manage (a nicer way of saying "control") your classroom, you are dead in the water.

These teachers would argue that there is no way to get anything done without good classroom management techniques; *no control* equals *no learning*.

And they're right! Classroom management is the single most important skill, especially for a new teacher.

So why then did I put the chapter on classroom management at the end of the book rather than the beginning?

Simple. Classroom management is just not that difficult. In fact, if you are applying the strategies and methods taught in this book so far, you are well on your way to mastering the skills of classroom management.

The truth is, the entire book could have been titled *Classroom Management*. Because, in fact, the entire book is about just that—*Classroom Management*.

As I stated in the introduction, the best *management system* is a strong *instructional system*.

Stopping Boredom

Now many new teachers will think that I must be crazy to say that managing your classroom is not difficult.

The fact is that the vast majority of discipline issues arise when students are bored or uninvolved in the lesson.

If you are using the strategies put forth in this book, you are going to greatly reduce your behavior problems. Here's why: *Students will be actively involved in your classroom.*

For example, the mini-lesson techniques described in Chapter 2 are a critical piece in the classroom management puzzle. When you break up your lessons into mini-blocks of learning in which you switch from one activity to another every ten minutes or so, your students will never get bored.

Here is a question every teacher interviewing for a job will hear from an interview committee: "How do you handle classroom management issues?"

Having sat on many interview committees I am amazed at how many teachers get this answer wrong.

Here is the correct answer: "I don't have many classroom management issues because my class is set up with a high degree of *mutual respect*, and students are always *actively involved* in the class. Because the students are not bored and are involved in the lesson, the chances of management problems are greatly reduced."

Now, as long as you can explain how your students are *actively involved*, what you mean by *mutual* respect, and what you will do on those rare occasions when management problems do arise...well then, you got yourself a job!!

Let's take a closer look at those three important factors: mutual respect, active involvement, and management "tricks."

1. Mutual Respect

I use the word "mutual" because we hear that word "respect" thrown around quite a bit in education.

The problem is that some teachers overlook the "mutual" part.

I don't think there is a teacher in the world that would disagree with me when I say that students must show respect toward their teachers. Unfortunately, some forget that teachers must also show the students respect.

Yes, *respect* is a two-way street. If you don't think so, get another job!!! (Sorry for being blunt...actually, no I'm not.)

The point is you will never get the respect of your students if you don't first show them respect yourself.

** That does NOT mean let the students do what they want. Actually, it is the exact opposite; students want to know what the limits are and they want those limits to be consistent!!

TIP#30: Consistency is essential if you are going to gain the respect of your students.

Here's what I did:

(Keep in mind I rarely, if ever, sent students to the principal's office. And no, I am not 6'6" and 220 pounds; I am only 5'7" and 155 pounds, and many of my students were actually bigger than I am.)

On the first day of school, like most teachers across America, I spent a fair amount of time establishing the rules of the classroom. I did this in a way that the students *thought* they were making up their own rules.

I started by telling them that we had one simple rule in the class, posted front and center above the front board: "Respect People, Respect Property."

I told them that I kept the rule simple and posted so everyone could remember it.

We then took a closer look at the *second* half of the rule and I explained what I meant by "respecting property."

I explained that I would never go through their stuff and never write on their things. They should respect the school's property by not writing on desks. I also explained what is specifically mine and said that they should not touch my stuff because everything had its place. Somehow my students came to call this "place" the other side of the "Line of Death." (Leave it to thirteen-year-olds to be overly dramatic.)

Nevertheless, students got the idea that other people's property is off-limits, including projects and class work.

We then focused on the first part of the rule, "Respect People." This is where I put everything on them and immediately started implementing the strategies of this book.

I told students that I absolutely expected them to show me the respect that I deserved, but they should also absolutely expect me to show them respect, and they should expect their classmates to respect one another.

I then had students take out a piece of paper and divide it into three columns. I gave them five (specific) minutes to write ways that they could show the teacher and one another respect and ways the teacher could show them respect. Just doing this activity created a great deal of mutual respect from day one. (Notice how I had already started to use the different strategies in this book, such as ON-THE-CLOCK, ALL WRITE, and of course I would always CHECK FOR UNDERSTANDING.)

Next, I had students PAIR/SHARE their ideas, while I used the INTERACTION SEQUENCE to determine who to call on.

Their ideas were great and gave a real insight into what they found respectful and disrespectful; for example, calling students' grades out, yelling, having teacher's pets are all things that you shouldn't be doing as a teacher.

Everyone knows the rules before they ever step foot into a classroom. For the most part, classroom rules are common sense. But here's what this activity did: By letting the students know that I was going to show *them* respect, and by actually taking the time to hear what they found respectful and disrespectful, I was able to accomplish a major goal right from day one: *I gained their respect*.

A friend of mine who was a successful builder in town helped our school by filling in as a technology teacher when we just could not find one. He was amazed at how much work went into teaching and gained a whole new respect for the profession. He kept asking me how I did it, and I simply told him, "It's all about respect. If you can get the students to respect you, it is absolutely amazing what you can get them to do. However, if they don't respect you, you can't get them to do anything."

2. Active Involvement

Since this entire book is about active involvement, there is no need to rehash everything that has been discussed thus far.

Once again, if students are actively involved in the class, they will not be bored.

If they are not bored, there will be significantly fewer problems.

If you are applying what has been taught in this book, then you are well on your way.

Remember: Be specific, be consistent, and check for understanding!!

3. Classroom Management "Tricks"

Of course you are going to have classroom management problems, even if you apply all these strategies; otherwise, you would be teaching in that "perfect world" that we discussed earlier.

So what do you do when problems arise?

Here is a helpful list of strategies:

- *Don't panic*

- *Don't Yell!! Don't Yell!! Don't Yell!!*

  If I could yell that at you I would.

  Never model bad behavior and yelling is bad behavior.

  Not only that, yelling is ineffective. If you constantly yell at your class, you lose the respect of your students and become just another voice in the crowd.

  Try doing just the opposite.

  That's right; when your students are starting to misbehave or are talking when they shouldn't be, say nothing, nothing at all. Just stand there and wait.

  Before you know it, the class will sense your displeasure and quickly respond. They will even tell each other to be quiet.

When all is said and done, you've regained control of your class without losing any respect (in fact, gaining more respect) and have done so in a timely manner (much quicker than yelling).

- *No Mass Punishment*

  This is obvious.

  How would you feel if you got in trouble for something that someone else did?

  I bet you would lose respect for the person who dealt out that punishment.

  Guess what? So will your students.

- *The Hierarchy*

  There are a series of steps you can take with students who are misbehaving.

  Start by shooting a glance toward the disruptive behavior. If that doesn't work, simply move closer to the disruption. If that doesn't work, give a general reminder of the rules. If that doesn't work, it's time for a "clinic."

- *The Clinic*
  (This strategy developed by APL Associates)

  This is one of the single most effective classroom management strategies I have ever seen or used.

  The clinic is a simple "retraining" of the expected behavior.

Here are the rules of the clinic:

1. Retraining is done on the student's valued time.

2. Retraining is done dispassionately. Don't get angry; the misbehavior is NOT PERSONAL. Just tell the student matter-of-factly, "Patricia, I would like to see you at recess today for a clinic."

3. A clinic should only be as long as it takes to reteach the behavior. I'd model the proper behavior once for the student and then have the student show me the appropriate behavior. This only takes a few minutes (clinics are not punitive).

4. Retrain as often as necessary. If you want it, you have to teach it.

The Clinic is an extremely successful classroom management strategy that is designed to help students be successful by working on self-control.

Here is an example of what happened when a couple of students did not do the *Do Now* when they came into class and instead decided to talk and joke with each other.

After shooting them glances and walking over to them failed to meet with any success, I simply said, "Eric and Ryan, I would like to see you today at recess for a *Do Now* clinic."

This is what followed at the recess clinic:

Teacher: "Hi guys, I just wanted to go over the procedures for starting class. Every day when you come into class, there is a *Do Now* on the board.

When you enter the room, you sit down at a desk, open your notebook, and write the answer to the question. Do you understand that?"

Students: "Yes, can we go now?"

Teacher: "Not yet. I just want to make sure you understand, so I am going to model it for you." (At this point I actually re-entered the room and sat at a desk and did the *Do Now*.)

Teacher: "Ok, now just to make absolutely sure, the two of you show me what you are going to do when you enter the room tomorrow." (At this point the students actually re-entered the room and did the *Do Now*.)

The whole process took less than five minutes. There was no yelling involved, just the minor inconvenience of missing some of recess.

Guess what these two students did the next day when they came into class? That's right; they did the *Do Now*.

Final Thoughts

Set your limits and stand your ground.

Studies prove that the part of the brain that makes good choices and rational decisions doesn't fully develop until ages twenty-one to twenty-five.

Students must be provided with ample opportunities to practice making rational decisions.

TIP#31: Be very cautious about rewarding behavior that students are supposed to be doing! This is not good practice! If you are going to reward positive behavior, make sure the reward is at the end of the task as a surprise and not at the front end as an expectation.

Remember: Extra credit should never used to allow students to get out of trouble!! (That would only reinforce the bad behavior.)

Chapter 11:

Closure

I decided to end this book, appropriately, with a chapter on closure, which is an important part of lessons.

You need to know if your objectives have been met by the end of each class. How else will you know if you did your job?

More importantly though, closure increases retention. It is through practice that we push things into our long-term memory.

There are many simple closure activities that can be used every day. Here are some examples:

- *Learning Log*

  While I didn't have students keep a daily learning log (where they write what they learned that day), I have seen them used with great success.

  Lisa Seff, a top-notch science teacher, had what she called the *Sum-It-Up*. It's like the opposite of the *Do Now*.

  Every day at the end of class, students filled out

their *Sum-It-Up* sheet in which they wrote at least one thing that they learned in class that day.

At the end of each week, students handed in their *Sum-It-Up* sheets for a quiz grade.

- *Pair/Share*

This is a quick and easy one. Have the students PAIR/SHARE the answer to a question that is based on the day's objectives.

- *Draw a picture*

- *Write a short journal entry*

This can be creative and also address the lesson's objectives.

For example: Write a journal entry from the perspective of an immigrant from the late 1800s. Your journal entry must include your experiences coming to the new world and specific "push-pull" factors that brought you here. (Explaining various "push-pull" factors that increased immigration in the late 1800s was one of our lesson's objectives.)

- *Write a letter*

This is similar to writing a journal entry. Be creative, but make sure to meet your objectives.

- *Create tomorrow's "Do Now"*

Have students use information from the day's lesson to create "Do Now" questions for tomorrow's class.

- *Write a dialogue*

  This doesn't necessarily have to be between two famous people.

  For example, I had students write a dialogue between a factory owner and a worker during industrialism. And, I made sure to have the students include several terms from our lesson on labor-management relations.

- *Create your own test*

  This is like a mini *Ticket-to-the-Test*. Have the students write a test question and answer for each of your lesson's objectives.

Basically, closure should tie up the lesson before you get the students started on their homework.

Oh yeah, that's right. You still have to get students to *start* the homework *in* class. (This is important—see Chapter 5: Homework.)

When you start putting it all together, you begin to realize that there is an awful lot to get done in a typical forty-five-minute period.

You must go through the *Agenda*, the *Objective*, and the *Do Now*. You must go over the homework using the INTERACTION SEQUENCE and CHECK FOR UNDERSTANDING (and, all of these before you even get to teaching new material).

Then, you must save enough time at the end of the period not only for closure, but also for getting the students started on their homework.

Welcome to the world of teaching, where your biggest enemy is *time*. That is why good time management skills are so critical to being a successful teacher.

Here is another time management tip: While many experts may disagree, I often combine my *closure activity* with my *homework*.

Think about it. If you are using homework assignments properly (see Chapter 5: Homework), they are basically the same as closure activities.

Both closure and homework activities are short assignments that are designed to reinforce what was taught in class.

Most of the closure activities above can easily be made into homework assignments.

Combining your closure activity with your homework assignment will definitely save you time. When you start your closure in class, you are also starting your homework.

I could still determine if my objectives were met by how well the students did on their homework assignment.

Remember: If you combine closure and homework, there is no excuse for not getting the activity started in class!!

The truth is, I really should have some closure activity for this book, but I have no way of holding you accountable.

Wouldn't it be funny if, as part of buying this book, you had to email me a journal entry as though you were a first year teacher implementing four strategies.

Don't worry! There is only so much you can learn from a book. In fact, this book is in no way meant to replace all the courses and professional development workshops that I have taken over the years. And, in no way is this book meant to replace experiences within the classroom.

Actually, the best thing you can do is start applying what you have learned from this book to your own classroom situation.

Start with one or two strategies and post them in the back of the classroom. After you master those, add one or two more.

Remember: Information is just information unless you do something with it!!

Final Thoughts

Education is a funny profession for a number of reasons:

- *There is a tremendous amount of research.*

- *There is no test group.*

- *Since there is no test group, educational research is easily manipulated.*

- You'll often hear teachers use the words "backed by research." I even used that line in this book. And yes, it is backed by research, but you can also find research to dispute almost anything in education.

The bottom line is this: Use your brain, do what works, and don't be afraid to test new and different teaching strategies.

Some strategies won't fit or feel right, others you may need to tweak to fit your own teaching style, and others you will simply be thrilled with from the first try.

I am truly convinced that if you apply these strategies in your own classroom you will see amazing results.

Chapter 12:

Teacher Resources

Here are the teacher resources that accompany this book. To download your bonus resources, visit: http:// thebusyeducator.com/effective

Curriculum Map from Chapter 2: Time Management

Classroom Management: The Proactive Approach A special report with proven strategies that will increase class participation, increase academic achievement, increase standardized test scores and decrease classroom management problems!

52 Teaching Tips Simple teaching tips and simple teaching strategies that are easy to apply to any classroom situation.

FREE Weekly Teaching Tips Newsletter This e-newsletter will provide you with simple teaching tips each and every week that you can easily apply in your very next class. Short timely tips that you can print out, post them in your classroom, and pass them around to other teachers. These tips are designed to be applied immediately.

One more thing…

Enjoyed This Book?

You Can Make A Difference

Thank you very much for purchasing this book *Become an Effective Teacher in Minutes: Best Teaching Practices You Can Use Now*. I'm very grateful that you chose this book from all the other wonderful books on the market.

I hope this book made your life as an elementary teacher that much more enjoyable for you and your students. If it did, please consider sharing your thoughts with your fellow teachers on Facebook, Twitter, LinkedIn and Instagram.

If you enjoyed this book and found value in reading it, please take few minutes to post an honest review for the book. Reviews are very important to readers and authors – and difficult to get. Reviews don't have to be long: even a sentence or two is a huge help. Every review helps.

While on your favorite review site, feel free to vote for helpful reviews. The top-voted reviews are featured for display, and most likely to influence new readers. You can vote for as many reviews as you like.

All the best,

Adam Waxler and Marjan Glavac